Golden Anniversary

Book of Devotions

by Cecil H. Skibbe

CTS FAMILY PRESS

Library of Congress Card Catalog Number: 01-000000

ISBN 1-930260-07-5

Golden Anniversary
Book of Devotions

The word ANNIVERSARY is made up of three Latin words;
1. "ANNI" means *"of the year"*
2. "VERS" means *"turning"*
3. "ARY" means *"connected with"*

So the word ANNIVERSARY means "connected with the turning of the year," and when the years have turned a certain number of times we have an anniversary.

The years have "turned," until the year 1997 was the fiftieth year of the graduation of Cecil H. Skibbe from Concordia Theological Seminary, Springfield, IL, and also the fiftieth year of the marriage of Cecil and Helen Lovekamp Skibbe.

Date of graduation: June 7, 1947
Date of marriage: June 8, 1947

Most of the devotions in this book were originally presented at various congregation, circuit and district meetings. Since these meditations grew over a period of nearly fifty years, it was not possible to determine the original source of some of the subject matter. However, since Herman W. Gockel has been the author's mentor and favorite writer of devotional material throughout his entire ministry, rest assured some of the thoughts and illustrations, originated from his pen. I am deeply indebted to Dr. Gockel, also for his special interest and encouragement in my humble writing efforts.

After the manuscript for this book was completed, word was received of Dr. Herman Gockel's homegoing on May 1, 1996. Dr. Gockel would have been 90 years on Oct. 11, 1996.

"Even to you old age, I am He, and even to gray hairs I will carry you! I have made, and I will bear; even I will carry, and will deliver you."

Isa. 46:4

Other Books by the Author

<u>**New and Old Treasures From the Storeroom**</u>
34 Sermons for special times and occasions.
14 original hymns to be sung with familiar tunes.
10 original prayers especially for mealtime.

<u>**Going Home Talk**</u>
A series of 28 special meditations
for Travelers, Pilgrims, Sojourners
who are ON THEIR WAY HOME
where Jesus has gone to prepare a place for us;
that place which is ours solely by grace
through faith in our blessed Savior.

Proceeds from the above books designated to the Cecil and Helen Skibbe Scholarship Endowment Fund established at Concordia Theological Seminary, Fort Wayne, Indiana, to assist young men in becoming pastors in The Lutheran Church-Missouri Synod.

Table of Contents

Dedicated to our Grandsons
Kevin, Timothy and Ryan

"For this reason I kneel before the Father, from whom his whole family in heaven and on earth derives its name. I pray that out of his glorious riches he may strengthen you with power through his Spirit in your inner being, so that Christ may dwell in your hearts through faith. And I pray that you, being rooted and established in love, may have power, together with all the saints, to grasp how wide and long and high and deep is the love of Christ, and to know this love that surpasses knowledge-that you may be filled to the measure of all the fullness of God.

"Now to him who is able to do immeasurably more than all we ask or imagine, according to his power that is at work within us, to him be glory in the church and in Christ Jesus throughout all generations, for ever and ever! Amen."

Eph. 3:14-21

Golden Anniversary

Book of Devotions

by Cecil H. Skibbe

Faithful at My Corner

A congregation was recognizing its 100th anniversary. It was a time of special celebration. One noon the chairman of the board of trustees came to the church to transact some business. As he approached the church he saw an elderly man carefully observing, and then patting the bricks at one corner of the church building. This intrigued the trustee of the congregation. He walked closer to the elderly man and spoke, "Pardon me sir, but I see you seem to have some special interest in this corner of the building. I'm an officer of the church, and I was wondering if you have some special memories?"

The elderly gentleman replied, "Yes, I have a special interest. You see, when this building was erected many years ago and I was still a young man, I was a workman on the project." Patting the bricks, he said, "I worked on this corner right here." And with a smile of satisfaction he continued, "I THINK I DID A PRETTY GOOD JOB." The trustee readily agreed. He had, indeed, done a PRETTY GOOD JOB.

The trustee went on to the church office and shared with the staff members the experience he had with the old man. It had a strange effect on them. For a moment they were silent and then it appeared that they all captured the nostalgic sense of satisfaction felt and expressed by the old gentleman. It seemed that the words kept repeating themselves. "I WORKED ON THIS CORNER, RIGHT HERE. I THINK I DID A PRETTY GOOD JOB."

As others heard the story, they began to ask

themselves, "On what corner have I worked in the ministry of this congregation represented in 100 years of its existence?"

There were solemn moments experienced by those who had served the Lord faithfully through the years. Some could visualize missionaries sent out to distant lands, and they could say, "Thank God I had the privilege of building on that corner with my words of encouragement, with my gifts and with my special prayers. That boy, that girl was in my Sunday school class and I was privileged to sow the precious seed of God's Word. Oh, yes, thank God, I was permitted and honored to work on that corner."

Another saw a Christian businessman, a mighty servant of the Lord, and remembered with deep gratitude to God that he had been privileged to lead him to the Lord through the guidance and power of the Spirit.

And there were others who could be identified as products of the work of God's faithful workmen: a Christian nurse, a teacher, a mother, a scout leader, several pastors who were given prayer and financial support while preparing for the ministry at the seminary. There were also several outstanding Christian physicians who were sons of the congregation, who had been faithfully fed spiritually by Word and Sacrament as they were growing up in their home church. Each of them were once boys and girls growing up in church, learning to love the Lord because the people of that past generation had been faithfully building on their respective corners.

The lesson became crystal clear. They began to realize that many corners still remained to be "worked on." Who would carry on?

If you, one day, want to touch a corner on which you faithfully worked, be sure to report for work today! *"Work while it is day, for the night comes when no one can work."* (John 9:4) The work must be done today for satisfaction tomorrow.

And the first, and most important corner for each of us to work is within the walls of our very own homes-faithfully teaching, guiding, encouraging-and with the Word of God and faithful prayer, building up those who have the same last name as we, living under the same roof with us. We begin with those and branch out from there.

Therefore, in the strength of the Lord, work faithfully and diligently now, so that you might be able to say one day, by the grace and mercy of a most benevolent God, I THINK WE DID A PRETTY GOOD JOB OF BEING FAITHFUL AT OUR CORNER!

O Holy Spirit, enter in,
And in our hearts YOUR WORK begin,
And make our hearts Your dwelling.
Sun of the soul, O Light divine,
Around and in us brightly shine,
Your strength in us up-welling.
In Your radiance Life from heaven
Now is given over-flowing,
Gift of gifts beyond all knowing.

Left to ourselves, we surely stray;
Oh, lead us on the narrow way,
With wisest counsel guide us;
And GIVE US FAITHFULNESS that we
May follow You forever free,
No matter who derides us.
Gently heal those hearts now broken;
Give some token You are near us,
Whom we trust to light and cheer us.

O mighty Rock, O Source of life,
Let Your good Word in doubt and strife
Be in us strongly burning
That WE BE FAITHFUL unto death
And live in love and holy faith,
From You true wisdom learning.
Lord, Your mercy on us shower;
By Your power Christ confessing,
We will cherish all Your blessing. Amen

LW 160

"We are to KEEP THE FAITH, but not to ourselves!"

Call for Me

Soon after I had entered the parish ministry, a veteran pastor asked me, "How are you doing?" I answered, "I guess I am doing the best I know how." He dropped his head and softly said, "I sure wish I would do the best I know how." Needless to say, I never gave that answer again!

All of which reminds me of the story of the young man who was spending his first day on a new job. Everything went well until shortly after noon when the machine he was operating began to make an unusual noise. Eager to demonstrate his mechanical ability he began to tinker with the machine—with the result that it soon came to a complete stop. Nothing that he could do would start the wheels in motion again.

Just then the foreman walked up. The young man, somewhat embarrassed but still trying to explain and defend his actions, told his superior exactly what he had done and then, shrugging his shoulders, added: "After all, I did my best!"

"Young man," the seasoned foreman replied as he looked the precocious novice squarely in the eye, "around here doing your best is to CALL FOR ME!"

What a lesson for our everyday living! He, in whose hands are all things and with whom nothing is impossible, would remind us: "Doing your best is to CALL FOR ME!" How often our Heavenly Father has had to remind us of that humbling, yet soul-strengthening fact! In our foolish pride we often think that we are doing our best when we apply our own puny wisdom to the difficult problems of daily living; and we so often forget that in the vexing trials and temptations of the Christian life, "doing our best is to CALL FOR HIM." How often we fail to do our best in school and in the work place and in our parenting and in our marriage and in our church life, simply because we often fail faithfully and diligently to CALL UPON THE LORD; to CALL UPON HIM to seek His guidance, help and blessing!

"CALL UPON ME" (Ps. 50:15) is still God's gracious command and glorious invitation to all of His followers. "I will help you, I will uphold you, I will deliver you" is still His precious promise, "And you shall glorify Me" is still His holy expectation.

A personal question: How often each day do you really CALL UPON THE LORD who so graciously promises to help us? "Pray and keep on praying," the Scriptures admonish and encourage us. May we, with the Psalmist, be able to say, "In the day of my trouble I CALL ON YOU, for You answer me" (Ps. 86:7). And then with the Psalmist vow to our blessed Lord, "Because He inclined His ear to me, therefore I WILL CALL ON HIM as long as I live" (Ps. 116:2).

No question about it, the Almighty Lord, in whose hands are all things and with whom nothing is impossible, would have us CALL FOR HIM and keep on calling. Oftentimes we "have not" and fail, simply because we do not faithfully CALL ON HIM who declares, "All power is given unto Me in heaven and on earth" (Matt. 28:18).

Remember the little boy who was trying to move a large rock? After watching him struggle for a little while his father asked, "Why don't you use ALL your strength?" The little boy got down and tried again, but could not move the rock. "Use all your strength," the father prodded. Trying again the little boy countered, "I am using all my strength!" "No, you're not," the father replied, "you haven't asked me yet!"

We do our best and use all our strength only when we faithfully CALL UPON THE LORD! CALL ON HIM RIGHT NOW!

My heart abounds in lowliness,
My soul with love is glowing,
And gracious words my lips express,
With meekness overflowing.
My heart, My mind, My strength, My all,
To God I yield, ON HIM I CALL.

TLH 421:3

We Pray to Jesus

The school nurse had just completed her health talk. There were still a few minutes for a brief review. "Tell me, Johnny," she said to a seven-year-old, "what is the first thing we do when we catch a cold?" Johnny rose to his feet and replied, in confident assurance: "We pray to Jesus!"

That wasn't exactly the answer the nurse expected, and for a moment she was at a loss for words. But only for a moment. For as she looked into the eager, confident face of little Johnny, she looked into a soul that was filled with faith; and before she knew it, she heard herself replying, "Yes, Johnny, we pray to Jesus."

Do your children have that kind of faith? Have you done everything in your power to cultivate an intimate friendship between your child and Christ?

Children who have been brought to Christ and kept with the Lord will talk to Him—also about their childhood illnesses, including a cold. Parents, dear parents, by example faithfully teach your children to PRAY TO JESUS.

"Those who stoop to help a child, stand tall."

Take Advantage of the Season

Presently our countryside is in brilliant array with the many different varieties of trees and their colored leaves on the hills and in the valleys of southern Indiana: Bloomington, Nashville, Brown County, along the Wabash to the Ohio River. What a beautiful spectacle! A short drive will provide many picturesque panoramas of gorgeous color. Even Solomon, in all his splendor, was not arrayed like southern Indiana in October. However, it will not last. It is only for a season. The glory will soon fade. You cannot delay your trip for any length of time and expect that the color will wait for your convenience. Now is the time. This will all slip away.

SO IT IS with many opportunities and occasions in life. If we neglect to seize the challenges and opportunities of the day or season, they may be gone forever.

Man looks to trees
For signs of
The moving seasons.

Soft greens and bursting buds of spring,
Leaves full and summer green,
Autumn's aging hues,
And dead leaves drift from barren winter limbs.

We see the tree's seasons as the stages
Of our lives from birth to death.

A fellow pastor gives us a touching example of opportunities getting away from us when he lovingly writes the following about his dear mother: "For long years she was a beautiful person—always doing things for others; interested in her children, grandchildren and even her great-grandchildren. It was good to share moments of life with her. However, the glory has faded. Although she is still alive, her health has deteriorated so that she no longer thinks about her family. Interesting conversations are no longer possible. The biggest challenge for her is to take a few more bites from her lunch tray. There is no more energy for baking, cooking, entertaining or visiting. IT IS LIKE A TREE WHOSE GLORY IS PAST."

But wait a minute, those forests and state park showcases which will soon be showing their bare limbs, without the special beauty which has attracted so much attention at this time, *are not really dead.* We can anticipate that there will be another springtime, another cycle of new buds and new fresh green leaves, and another display of glorious color.

And isn't it true, we have a similar anticipation for ourselves and for our loved ones—an anticipation far more splendid and glorious than words can describe? Although in this present season of our lives strength gives way to weakness, beauty and intelligence fade, and eventually life gives way to death, nevertheless, we joyfully, confidently anticipate a new life! We eagerly expect and fully trust a glorious resurrection from the grave to a new, blessed, eternal life with the holy Lord God!

This new and eternal, glorious life is ours solely by grace through faith in Christ, God's Son, who lived and died and rose again for us. Give attention to the promise of our blessed Savior. He promises: "I am the Resurrection and the life. Whoever believes in Me will live, even though he dies . . ." (John 11:25f.).

Our Savior Redeemer further promises us: "I go to prepare a place for you; I will come back and take you to Myself, so that you will be where I am" (John 14:3). We can rest assured that it will be a beauty and glory far beyond anything we have known during our season of life here on earth. How blessed!

A final thought and reminder: Many of you have parents who can still bring joy and happiness into your life; they are parents who also need the attention and love that only you can give them. You can delay and wait for a convenient season; but you cannot wait forever. The glory will fade. TAKE ADVANTAGE OF THE SEASON!

And so it was a tree
On which our Savior
Bled and died
To give us life
That never ends.

As new buds bloom
From winter limb
Season after season,
So God's children move
From life to death
To life eternal.

When Empty Means Full

(The following, although it has been rephrased and condensed, remains a true story.)

His classmates noted that eight-year-old Stephen's mental retardation was becoming more manifest. Could they retain their love for him as they came to see his difference more each day? In April their Sunday school teacher asked all eight children in the class to hide within an empty L'eggs pantyhose container one small object that represented the new life of spring.

Fearing that Stephen might not have caught on and not wishing to embarrass him, the teacher had the children place all unlabeled containers on her desk so she could open them. The first container had a tiny flower. What a lovely sign of new life! The donor could not help but erupt, "I brought that one!"

Next came a rock. That must be Stephen's, since rocks don't symbolize life. But Billy shouted out that his rock had moss on it and moss represented new life. The teacher agreed. A butterfly flew from the third container, and the butterfly was the best choice to symbolize new life. The fourth L'eggs container was empty. "It has to be Stephen's," thought the teacher, reaching for the fifth container. But "Please don't skip mine," Stephen interjected. "But it's empty!" said the teacher. "That's right," said Stephen. "The tomb was empty on Easter, and that's NEW LIFE FOR EVERYONE."

14

Later that summer Stephen's condition worsened and he died. At his funeral, on the casket, the mourners found eight L'eggs pantyhose containers, now ALL empty.

"In truth, in very truth, I tell you, a grain of wheat remains a solitary grain unless it falls into the ground and dies; but if it dies, it bears a rich harvest."

(John 12:24)

Fix Our Hearts
and Eyes on Jesus

Recently a number of people have shared with me their experiences of attending "church services" which were very different from that to which they were accustomed. One simply said, "I was entertained, but I really didn't worship because of all the ornate processions and various forms of ostentatious chancel prancing. The Lord Jesus was not the center and focus of the gathering."

Another spoke of the music—especially of the words which were anything but Christ-centered, and the same was said of the leader's message. The blessed Savior was not the central Figure of the worship.

Of course, there are always those who will try to defend such "services" by saying, "But look how many people they are reaching!" I want to ask, "For what, and especially for whom are they reaching these people?" That question is usually countered with, "But obviously they are giving the people what they want!" To which we must ask: "Do we always go the way of Almighty God or the Gallup polls?"

This is an apt illustration of modern mankind who has both feet firmly planted in midair! So many don't know where they are going, but they are making good time. They go through life trying to satisfy their personal appetites. Finally, however, they run out of fuel and die. As long as they do not know whose they are and where they are going, they are lost—really lost! A navigator is lost unless he can "fix" on some solid object, and so is mankind.

How do ice skaters keep their balance as they spin on the ice? They "fix their eyes" on one spot and return to it with each whirl. As long as they do that, they can keep spinning on and on. However, if they lose their point of focus, they fall. So it is with mankind.

A number of pastors were meeting at a state park lodge. As we were being seated in the dining hall for lunch, one of the waitresses said softly, "This is my first day at work here and I am very nervous." A little later, she was having difficulty serving coffee without having some of it spill in the saucer before setting it down for the customer. Another waitress advised: "Don't look down at the coffee; it will throw you off balance. Keep your eyes on your destination."

That works in life as well. We must keep our hearts and eyes on our destination. Unless we FIX OUR HEARTS AND EYES ON JESUS AND ETERNAL LIFE THROUGH HIM, we will lose our spiritual balance. That is why God sent Jesus, to be the "fix" for us so that we might clearly know where we are, and whose we are, and where we are going.

After all, Jesus *"came to seek and to save that which was lost,"* and this He fully accomplished by His suffering and death on the cross and His glorious resurrection from the grave on that first Easter Morn. And He it is who declares: *"I am the Way, the Truth and the Life. No one comes to the Father but by Me"* (John 14:6). *"Follow Me!"* Jesus bids.

We need only remember how responsive our Lord Jesus was to our need when we were dead in sin; how concerned He was about our plight; how diligent He was in pursuing us when we were lost; how He spared no cost to redeem us, even sacrificing life itself so we might live.

It is that glorious truth which generates in us the response of repentance, trust in the gracious Lord who forgives us, love for Him who so loved us, and the ability to consecrate ourselves to His service and to the service of others.

In that connection there is no better word to stir us to action than what the writer to the Hebrews says.

After appealing to us to remember the example of the believers who have gone before us, he says: *"Let us throw off everything that hinders and the sin that so easily entangles, and let us run with perseverance the race marked out for us. LET US FIX OUR EYES ON JESUS, the Author and PERFECTER of our faith, who for the joy set before Him endured the cross, scorning its shame, and sat down at the right hand of the throne of God. Consider Him who endured such opposition from sinful men, so that you will not grow weary and lose heart"* (Heb. 12:1-3).

Therefore, all who, through the power of the Holy Spirit, FIX THEIR HEARTS AND EYES ON JESUS, will reach their eternal destination safely.

In the meantime, our privilege is to tell others about the blessed Lord Jesus, the only Savior of mankind. We can say it this way: God wants you to FIX YOUR HEART AND EYES ON JESUS.

He wants you to know that you came from Him and you will never find true happiness until you return to Him. Jesus, alone, can steer your life to your heavenly Father. Then you will not be lost, and you will truly know who you are, whose you are and where you are going.

Hymn 155 in *The Lutheran Hymnal* states it beautifully:

Sweet the moments, rich in blessing,
Which before the cross we spend,
Life and health and peace possessing
From the sinners' dying Friend.

Here we rest in wonder, viewing
All our sins on Jesus laid;
Here we see redemption flowing
From the sacrifice He made.

Here we find the dawn of heaven
While upon the cross we gaze,
See our trespasses forgiven,
And our songs of triumph raise.

Oh, that, near the cross abiding,
We may to the Savior cleave,
Naught with Him our hearts dividing,
All for Him content to leave!

Lord, in loving contemplation
FIX OUR HEARTS AND EYES ON THEE
Till we taste Thy full salvation
And Thine unveiled glory see. Amen.

It's Better Higher Up

The people of Israel waited expectantly for the promised Messiah, and the Early Church waited expectantly for His return.

The Christian life is an *expectant life*. It is a life lived in anticipation that the promises of God will all be fulfilled. No matter what our situation may be today, regardless of how dark or how depressing the weather outside, regardless of how hurtful or stressful our situation may be on the inside, we anticipate that our God will most definitely fulfill His promises—each and every one of them. He will provide for us and care for us day by day. He has promised, and He always keeps His promises—every one of them.

Dwight L. Moody used to tell a story about an optimistic and cheerful lady who was, nonetheless, a shut-in, bedridden in an attic apartment on the fifth floor of a rundown building. There was no elevator in the building and there she was, lying alone in a shabby room of this rundown apartment building.

One of her friends came to see her one day and brought with her another friend, who was from a wealthy family. They wanted to cheer up this bedridden lady.

As they entered the building the wealthy visitor was struck by the depressing surroundings. As they mounted the stairs to the second floor it was almost more than she could handle. "Such a dark, depressing and filthy place," she said to her friend.

Her friend responded, "It's better higher up!"

They climbed the stairs to the third landing. "It's even worse here," she said. Her friend responded, "It's better higher up!"

Finally they got to the fifth floor and entered the dear lady's apartment, tiny and rundown. But the lady's face was glowing to see her friend, and she was radiating with the love of the Lord Jesus in her heart.

The wealthier woman could not ignore the awful surroundings, and she said in a sympathetic way, "It must be most difficult for you to be living here like this."

The lady smiled knowingly and said, "Yes, but it's better higher up."

That's the promise by which Christians live. "It's better higher up."

How wonderful it is to look forward to the fulfillment of God's promises, and what promise could be better at the beginning of a new year or the beginning of each new day, than the greatest promise ever made, *"For God so loved the world that He gave His one and only Son, that whoever believes in Him shall not perish but have eternal life"* (John 3:16).

As we continue to look forward with joyful expectation to the fulfillment of the many promises of God, let us never forget His great love for us and His promise that as we believe in Him we will indeed have the greatest gift He could ever give—the gift of EVERLASTING LIFE—A HOME WITH HIM IN HEAVEN. To be sure, IT'S BETTER HIGHER UP!

I'm but a stranger here,
Heav'n is my home;
Earth is a desert drear,
Heav'n is my home.
Danger and sorrow stand
Round me on ev'ry hand;
Heav'n is my fatherland,
Heav'n is my home.

Therefore I murmur not,
Heav'n is my home;
Whate'er my earthly lot,
Heav'n is my home;
And I shall surely stand
There at my Lord's right hand.
Heav'n is my fatherland,
Heav'n is my home.

TLH 660:1,4

Shut In

Shut-in . . . I never liked the word—
It held a plaintive note
Until a different view I got
From what one shut-in wrote:

"Shut in?" she said . . . "Oh, yes, indeed
Shut in from noise and strife . . .
But shut out are so many things
That cluttered up my life;

Shut in are peace and faith and hope . . .
Shut out are fear and doubt;
Shut in are words and deeds of cheer
No heart can do without.

Shut in my mind are memories
Of happier, brighter years;
I laugh, sometimes, remembering . . .
Sometimes I yield to tears . . .

Shut in are friends I cannot lose—
I hold them in my heart;
And though the miles stretch long between,
We never are apart!

SHUT-IN . . . why, it's a blessed word!
My soul will one day trod
On happy feet to heaven's door
And be SHUT IN . . . WITH GOD!"

Author Unknown

"Prayer doesn't necessarily change THINGS for us, but it changes US for things."

Our God Is Available

The boys and girls in confirmation class were each asked to name an attribute of God. One after the other named an attribute: eternal, unchangeable, omnipotent, omniscient, omni-present, holy, just, faithful, benevolent, merciful—and now it was Tim's turn. The attributes of God that had come to Tim's mind had already been named. Finally, in near desperation, Tim ventured, "Available!"

"Available" was not one of the attributes mentioned in the Catechism, but the alert and understanding teacher was quick to reply: "Yes, Tim, 'available' is one of the most wonderful attributes of our God!"

Perhaps Tim didn't realize it at the time, but the Lord's AVAILABILITY to all of us is definitely one of His most important and most significant characteristics. No matter what the condition or situation, day or night, summer or winter, whether young or old, it makes no difference, the Lord God is always AVAILABLE to us. His door is always open to us. He has no set office hours. He is always ready, willing and able to serve us. He is always waiting to hear from us.

It is not so with anyone else. Our telephone service was interrupted. We could neither receive nor make calls. I called from our neighbors' and talked to all kinds of people with the telephone company in all parts of the country trying to have our service restored. For four days no one was available to help us.

I contacted our furnace company to have our furnace

checked. That was two weeks ago. We have a promise, but to date no one is available.

How often one can wait for hours to see a doctor. They are not always available to us. They may have an emergency or are seeing another patient or they are in surgery or on vacation. We also experience having appointments cancelled because someone is unavailable to us.

Not so with our Lord and Savior. He has, as it were, a WALK-IN sign on the throne room of His Father. That is what St. Paul meant when he wrote: *"Therefore, being justified by faith, we have peace with God through our Lord Jesus Christ, by whom also WE HAVE ACCESS by faith into this grace wherein we stand" (Rom. 5:1-2).*

As believers in the Lord Jesus Christ, WE HAVE CONSTANT ACCESS into the presence of our Heavenly Father. He is available to anyone and everyone who, in faith, calls on Him morning, noon and night. *"There is not a moment when His eyes are not upon the righteous and His ears open to their prayers." (1 Pet. 3:12)*

With outstretched arms His age-old invitation is still the same: *"Call upon Me in the day of trouble; I will deliver you, and you shall glorify Me (Ps. 50:15).* He is waiting for us to call. As a matter of fact He promises: *"Before you call I will answer, and while you are yet speaking, I will hear"* (Isa. 65:24). He longs to have you come to Him. With outstretched arms He bids: *"Come unto Me all you who labor and are heavy laden and I will give you rest"* (Matt. 11:28). He is waiting to hear from you!

Talk about AVAILABILITY! Listen: *"Fear not FOR I AM WITH YOU, be not dismayed, for I am your God; I will strengthen you, I will help you, I will uphold you with My victorious right hand"* (Isa. 41:10). Furthermore, Jesus says to those who have kept His Word and have not denied His name, *"Behold, I have set before you an OPEN DOOR, which no one is able to shut"* (Rev. 3:8). The Apostle Paul reminds us: *"We have boldness and confidence of ACCESS THROUGH OUR FAITH IN CHRIST JESUS OUR LORD"* (Eph. 3:12). May we never forget: *"The eyes of the Lord are upon the righteous, and His ears are OPEN TO OUR PRAYERS"* (1 Pet. 3:12). Take this beautiful, soul-strengthening truth to heart, for there is none other so AVAILABLE to us as is our Lord and Savior, Jesus Christ. *"If I take the wings of the morning and dwell in the uttermost parts of the sea, even there Thy hand shall lead me, and Thy right hand shall hold me."* (Ps. 139:9-10)

Tim may have been groping for an attribute of God, but he could not have hit upon a better one than AVAILABLE to describe the Lord of heaven and earth.

What a blessed source of comfort, courage and strength to know that our precious Savior, in whose hands are all things and with whom nothing is impossible, is ALWAYS AVAILABLE to us! He truly has the EVER OPEN DOOR policy.

How good it is to remember, to pray and to sing:

TODAY THY MERCY CALLS US
To wash away our sin.
However great our trespass,
Whatever we have been,
However long from mercy
Our hearts have turned away,
Thy precious blood can cleanse us
And make us white today.

TODAY THY GATE IS OPEN,
And all who enter in
Shall find a Father's welcome
And pardon for their sin.
The past shall be forgotten,
A present joy be giv'n,
A future grace be promised,
A glorious crown in heav'n.

TODAY OUR FATHER CALLS US,
His Holy Spirit waits;
His blessed angels gather
Around the heav'nly gates.
No question will be asked us
How often we have come;
Although we oft have wandered,
It is our Father's home.

O all-embracing Mercy,
O EVER OPEN DOOR,
What should we do without Thee
When heart and eye run o'er?
When all things seem against us,
To drive us to despair,
We know ONE GATE IS OPEN,
One ear will hear our prayer. Amen.

TLH 279

God's Word Is Truth

There are many truths in the Scriptures that our human nature does not like to hear and that our human reason oftentimes resents. For example, we do not like to hear the Law which condemns us as sinners and tells us that there is no good in us by nature. After all, isn't there some good in everyone, and God should not condemn us for that? (Note Rom. 3:23 and Matt. 15:19.)

We do not like to hear that our God is a God of justice who in wrath will punish the unbelieving and impenitent. After all, isn't He a God of love who will overlook sin and save all who sincerely try to do their best? True, God is love, but He is also a just God, and justice demands of Him to punish the evildoer.

Furthermore, we do not like to hear that our rebellion against God was so serious that it required nothing less than the shedding of the blood of the Son of God for our redemption and forgiveness. Many people ridicule that as a crude and cruel "blood theology."

Or how about those who resent the fact that God created all things, but insist that everything that exists evolved by a process of natural selection?

How about those who reject the fact that we must call willful abortion murder, or those who argue that homosexuality, which God calls an abomination, is a permissible life-style?

We could go on! The point is that there are many things God has clearly stated but that sinful human nature does not like to hear. People criticize the Bible as being outdated. After all, they say, those who wrote the Bible lived at a time that did not have the advantages of our enlightened, scientific age.

But who gives us the right to sit as judges over the truth of Scripture? By doing that, we would be the self-appointed judges over God Himself. We would be telling the Almighty God: "You should not have done this or that. You should have done and said things differently." (Note Gal. 6:7.)

Dare we challenge God like that? The Apostle Paul asks, *"Who has known the mind of the Lord? Or who has been His counselor? Or who has first given to Him, and it shall be recompensed to him again?"* (Rom. 11:34-35). The fact is that God severely rebuked Job for questioning His wisdom and His ways.

The way some people question and criticize God and His holy, inspired Word of truth reminds one of the story of two taxidermists who stopped before a window where an owl was displayed. They immediately began to criticize the way the owl was mounted. Its eyes were not natural. The wings were not in proportion with the head. The feathers were not neatly arranged. The feet could certainly be improved.

When they had finished their criticism, the owl turned his head . . . and winked at them!

Thank God HIS WORD IS TRUTH! (John 17:17) If that were not the case, we could not be sure of a thing. Above all, we could not be certain of our salvation.

However, by the grace and mercy of a just, benevolent, patient, loving Lord and Savior, we know the Holy Scriptures, given by inspiration of God, *"are able to make us wise unto salvation through faith which is in Christ Jesus,"* and are profitable for our whole life as children of

God (2 Tim. 3:15-16). May we as individuals and as families faithfully be in the Word.

God's Word is our great heritage
And shall be ours forever;
To spread its light from age to age
Shall be our chief endeavor.
Through life it guides our way,
In death it is our stay.
Lord, grant, while worlds endure,
We keep its teachings pure
Throughout all generations. Amen.

TLH 283

"Oh Lord, sanctify us by the truth; YOUR WORD IS TRUTH."   AMEN

How to Defend the Bible

I am the Bible. I am God's wonderful library.
 I am always—and above all—THE TRUTH.

To the weary pilgrim,
 I am a good, strong Staff.

To the one who sits in black gloom,
 I am glorious Light.

To those who stoop beneath heavy burdens,
 I am sweet Rest.

To him who has lost his way,
 I am a safe Guide.

To those who have been hurt by sin,
 I am healing Balm.

To the discouraged,
 I whisper a glad message of Hope.

To those who are distressed by the storms of life,
 I am a safe Anchor.

To those who suffer in lonely solitude,
 I am a soft Hand resting upon a fevered brow.

O child of man, TO BEST DEFEND ME,
 FAITHFULLY USE ME!

Holy Spirit More Learned

Recently I read of some theologians who can't quite sell Genesis, chapters 1 and 2 down the river and yet they want to buy some evolution. Those tempted might recall these lines of Luther:

"I have often said that whoever would study Holy Scripture should be sure to see to it that he stays with the clear words as long as he can and by no means depart from them unless an article of faith compels him to understand them differently. For of this we must be certain:

"No clearer speech has been heard on earth than what God has spoken. Therefore, when Moses writes that God created heaven and earth and whatever is in them in six days, then let this remain six days, and do not venture to devise any comment that six days were one day or a long period of time.

"But if you cannot understand how this could have been done in six days, then grant the Holy Spirit the honor of being MORE LEARNED THAN YOU ARE.

"Remember, God gave us the Bible as a comfort and a support, not as a topic for debate. Never put a question mark where God puts a period."

Deo Volente

(God-Willing)

The good Lord willing was a phrase that our dear friend, Edna, used repeatedly in her everyday conversation. It is not unusual for me to use that phrase, or simply to use the letters, D.V., in my correspondence.

We have all heard graduation speeches and motivational seminars where we are told, "You can reach the sky." The intention is to inspire higher goals and greater ambition. While we appreciate encouragement, as Christians we are wary of assurances and goal-setting that leaves our Lord and Savior out of the picture.

It would be difficult to express it more clearly and to the point than St. James does when he writes: *"Now listen, you who say, 'Today or tomorrow we will go to this or that city, spend a year there, carry on business and make money.' Why, you do not even know what will happen tomorrow. What is your life? You are a mist that appears for a little while and then vanishes. Instead, you ought to say, 'IF IT IS THE LORD'S WILL (Deo Volente), we will live and do this or that'"* (James 4:13-15).

St. James noted that even we Christians at times are tempted to make plans without considering the will of the Lord. He reminds us that we who live under a loving God depend on His good pleasure. When we plan for the future, we must seek guidance and direction from Him. When we add "God-willing," we are doing much more than tacking on a pious phrase. The words, GOD-

WILLING, express our willingness to change or even abandon OUR plans in favor of GOD's WILL.

We cannot help but note that in the beautiful, model prayer that our God and Father has given to us, we have these words: "THY WILL be done on earth as it is in heaven." The Catechism asks and answers:

"What does this mean? The good and gracious will of God is done indeed without our prayer; but we pray in this petition that it may be done among us also. And what is the good and gracious will of God? The good and gracious will of God is that we hallow His name and that His kingdom come. What does the good and gracious will of God include? This good and gracious will of God includes: Everything that God wants to do for us according to His promise; Everything that God wants us to do and to avoid according to His will; Everything that God wants us to suffer patiently according to His good pleasure" (Luther's Small Catechism, 1971 edition, pages 156 and 157).

My favorite author of devotional material, Herman Gockel, once wrote about an elderly woman who lay sick in a hospital. Her talkative visitor went to great lengths to express her sympathy. "It's a shame this had to happen to you"—and so on and on.

Finally, the woman in bed interrupted. "Ellen, I don't see it that way at all. I'm getting what I asked for." The astounded visitor stood speechless as the Christian patient continued: "For many years I've been ending my evening prayers with the brief petition, 'Nevertheless, NOT MY WILL BUT THINE BE DONE.' The way I see it, my present illness is part of God's answer to that prayer.

It's His will that's being done. And if my present illness is part of His will for me, I know it's for my best."

How many of us have learned to look upon our crosses as evidences of God's good and gracious will toward us? Isn't it true that frequently when we pray "not my will but Thine be done," we do so under mild protest as though God's will were something ungracious and unkind?

We who have seen the God of heaven in the face of Jesus Christ need not be afraid of committing our lives entirely and completely to His will, because we know that His will toward us is one of love and mercy. Through Christ we know that God is on our side. And the God who sacrificed His own Son to redeem us will not let us down ever! As the Apostle Paul declares: *"If God be for us, who can be against us? He that spared not His own Son, but delivered Him up for us all, how shall He not with Him also freely give us all things?"* (Rom. 8:31f.).

For the believer to pray "not my will but Thine be done" is to ask for the fruition of everything good that God has planned for us. If we know, as we do know, that God in ages past has chosen us to live with Him in eternal bliss and glory, then surely we shall be able to look upon even our crosses as part and parcel of His grace and mercy. (Note: Rom. 8:28-39) We shall be happy to "get what we ask for"—the fulfillment of His holy, good and gracious will.

In days of illness, in days of sorrow, in moments of dark anxiety and deep distress, the believer in the Lord Jesus Christ can still pray with assurance:

What God ordains is always good:
HIS WILL IS JUST AND HOLY.
As he directs my life for me,
I follow meek and lowly.
My God indeed in ev'ry need
Knows well how he will shield me;
To him, then, I will yield me.

LW 422:1

Mourning in the Evening

In my office is a white porcelain dove on a black pedestal, a gift from my Sunday school staff of 25 years ago. As you know, there are a number of references to the dove in the Scriptures. Doves were sold in the temple courts—used for sacrifices (Lev. 12:6,8; Luke 2:24; Mark 11:15). On three different occasions Noah sent forth a dove from the ark (Gen. 8:8f.). The dove is used as the symbol of the Holy Spirit (Matt. 3:16; Mark 1:10; Luke 3:22; John 1:32). Other references to the dove: Gen. 15:9; Lev. 12:6; Ps. 55:6, 68:13 and 74:10.

The dove is a symbol of gentleness and innocence, faithful to its mate, and home-loving. Because of its nature and low, soft cooing sound, the dove is often referred to as the mourning dove.

In Isaiah 59:11 we read, *"we moan and moan like doves."* And because of sin we have every reason to moan, grieve, lament, to be sad and to mourn. Thus the title of this meditation: MOURNING IN THE EVENING.

"The old sinful nature in us should, by daily contrition (sorrow for sins) and repentance, be drowned and die with all sins and evil lusts." (Luth. Catechism, p. 178f.) In other words, as the sun sets and evening shadows crowd out the last light of each day, the darkness of the night about us becomes the symbol of mourning. Each nightfall descends slowly and gently as a divine reminder, repent! repent! repent!

Repentance is and always must be one of the most important characteristics of a Christian life. Repentance, defined in a wide sense, is being truly sorry for our sins, confessing our sins to God, and then receiving the blessed forgiveness of sins through our Lord Jesus Christ. We think of the words of Job when he said, *"I despise myself, and repent in dust and ashes"* (Job 42:6).

We remember that we are but dust and to dust our bodies shall return.

Jesus Christ's message was a message of repentance. *"Repent, for the kingdom of heaven is at hand."* (Matt. 4:17) His ministry was a ministry to and for sinners. He said, *"I have not come to call the righteous, but sinners to repentance"* (Luke 5:32). Later, in Mark, chapter 6, Christ called the twelve together, charged them with the specifics of their mission, and verse 12 reads: *"So they went out and preached that all should REPENT."*

At the very end of His earthly ministry Christ summed up His ultimate, climactic charge to His disciples, just before His glorious ascension into heaven, saying that in His name the message of *"REPENTANCE and the FORGIVENESS OF SINS must be preached to all nations."*

REPENT is a HARSH word. It bores into the very core of things, and it stabs the heart. Repent, change! But we resist change. We do not want to change our minds, either about things, ideas or people. There is as much irony as there is humor in the saying, "I've made up my mind. Please don't disturb me with the facts!"

But the facts are disturbing! I have sinned this day in thought, desire, word and deed. I have committed sins of omission and sins of commission. I have nurtured my prejudices. I have cherished my opinionated notions about my importance. I have resisted forgiving my offenders. I have gloried in excelling on my own terms. I should have shepherded, but I herded instead. Even though I have feet of clay, I enjoyed stepping on the toes of others. I had a chance to say a kind word, but my preoccupation with my own little shriveled world blinded my eyes and stilled my voice to a brother's or a sister's need.

"Repent" is a word with STING in it. But there is also balm, for it is an INVITING word. It is an invitation to be changed more into the likeness of Jesus, God's own Son, our blessed Lord and Savior. It is a summons to mercy and a welcome to forgiveness.

"Repent" is also a WOOING word of the winsome Spirit of God—whispering, pleading, begging, crying, calling: "Come back to Him who is the Way, the Truth and the Life."

Oh, yes, "Repent" is a harsh word, a disturbing word. "Repent" is a word with sting in it alright, but it is an inviting word as well.

Also, "Repent" is the BEST word at the end of each day. For this MOURNING IN THE EVENING is transformed into joy and blessing by the God of all grace. What does He do?

He exchanges our sins for His righteousness.
He exchanges our ugliness for His beauty.
He exchanges our guilt for His innocence.
He exchanges our death for His life.
He exchanges hell for His heaven.
He says: "Be of good cheer.
Your sins are forgiven you."

May we always be reminded of the bitterness and the sweetness of repentance brought about by faithful MOURNING IN THE EVENING.

Are You Weary,
Dear Brother, in the Ministry?

It is spiritually refreshing to know that our Savior was human enough to grow weary. There were times when He chose to do nothing but to rest awhile.

As you know, the Office of the Holy Ministry is an exacting one and makes demands that leave the faithful servant of the Word physically and mentally limp at times. There is a ceaseless rat-a-tat against his spiritual armor. The devil plagues him. His flesh wars against his spirit. The world nibbles at his spiritual vitals.

A severe temptation confronts the hard-working herald of the Cross when he becomes weary. It is a blessed thing if he becomes tired IN service. But then he is tempted to become tired OF service. The dark thoughts of suspicion, futility, self-pity and anger engulf him. Like Elijah, he pouts under the juniper tree and wishes he could die.

The place to lie down when weary at heart is not under the juniper tree, but rather under the tree of the Cross. There we find rest for our souls and reason enough to thank God for being permitted the honor of becoming tired IN serving. There, under the shadow of the Cross, we can repent of becoming tired OF serving. There, under the shadow of the Cross we can be enfolded by "the everlasting arms" of our blessed Savior and hear Him say: *"Do you not know? Have you not heard? The Lord is the everlasting God, the Creator of the ends of the earth. He will not grow tired or weary, and His understanding no one can fathom. He gives strength to the weary and increases the power of the weak. Even youths grow tired and weary, and young men stumble and fall; but those who hope in the Lord will renew their strength. They will soar on wings like eagles; they will run and not grow weary, they will walk and not be faint"* (Isa. 40:28-31).

Lord of the Church, we humbly pray
for those who guide us in Your way
and speak Your holy Word.
With love divine their hearts inspire
and touch their lips with hallowed fire,
and needful strength afford. Amen.

Endings and Beginnings

Life is filled with ENDINGS AND BEGINNINGS:

-the END of one day and the BEGINNING of another.

-the END of the shower and the BEGINNING of the
    sunshine.

-the ENDING AND BEGINNING of a week, a month and
    a year.

-the END of a semester and the BEGINNING of the
    second.

-the ENDING of one responsibility and the BEGINNING
    of a new task and challenge.

-November marks the END of a Church Year;

December marks the BEGINNING of another.

-our calendar year ENDS December 31,

and a new year BEGINS January 1.

ENDINGS AND BEGINNINGS, good days and bad, change and decay, joy and sorrow—of such is our life composed. None of us know how many days or years of grace remain for us.

Every year brings changes; changes in both our spiritual and physical life. Spiritually, our faith becomes stronger or weaker. Our love grows warmer or colder. Our commitment to Christ increases or decreases. Physically we all get older. Our children grow up and leave home. For some, illness weights us down. For others, death separates us from loved ones. For still others, a house is exchanged for an apartment or a bed in a nursing home.

Some changes bring gladness; others cause pain. Some changes bring joy; others bring tears and heartache. Through it all the clock of time keeps ticking. The pages on the calendar are turned one after another.

How has it been for you in your life with God the past year? Is your faith stronger or weaker than it was a year ago? Are you now closer to your Lord or further away from Him? If further away, remember, He hasn't moved or changed!

The Psalmist thought about all these things—the ENDINGS AND BEGINNINGS—and by inspiration wrote: *"You sweep men away in the sleep of death; they are like the new grass of the morning—though in the morning it springs up new, by evening it is dry and withered"* (Ps. 50:5,6).

While there are many things we do not know, what we do know in all these ENDINGS AND BEGINNINGS is that the Lord our GOD DOES NOT CHANGE! He declares: *"I am the Lord, I change not"* (Mal. 3:16). *"He is the same yesterday, today and forever."* (Heb. 13:8) Though we cannot fathom it with our puny and limited minds, God, our God, is eternal—without beginning and without end. He is from everlasting to everlasting. The Psalmist declares: *"Lord, Thou hast been our dwelling place in all generations. Before the mountains were brought forth, or ever Thou hadst formed the earth and the world, FROM EVERLASTING TO EVERLASTING THOU ART GOD"* (Ps. 90:1,2).

How do we handle all the ENDINGS AND BEGINNINGS? The words of Moses to God's people in his day have been preserved for all of God's people today: *"Be strong and of good courage, do not fear or be afraid, for it is the Lord your God WHO GOES WITH YOU;*

HE WILL NOT FAIL YOU OR FORSAKE YOU" (Deut. 31:7). With the Psalmist we can joyfully and confidently say: *"My times are in Your hands"* (Ps. 31:15).

Our friend, Marian, knew that beautiful truth, that her times were in the hands of the Lord. She had asked my wife and me to stop at her apartment as she was scheduled for surgery in the next couple days. The doctors had carefully explained to her the seriousness of the surgery. Marian told us, "My times are in the hands of the Lord, so if after the surgery I awake here on earth or in heaven, either way I'm a winner!" What a precious comfort! In health or in sickness, in joy or in sorrow, in life or in death, both of them—Jesus and she—would always be together. During the surgery the Lord took Marian to Himself.

Our life is ordered and regulated by the Lord God, our Heavenly Father. And God dearly loves us. He loved us so much that He gave His only-begotten Son to redeem us through His cross on Calvary. And now, no matter where we are, whatever our days may bring—no matter what the ENDINGS AND BEGINNINGS may be—we are in the Heavenly Father's hands and in His safekeeping, and no one can pluck us out of His hands, for He is the Almighty One of heaven and earth (John 10:27-29). Therefore, through the power of the Holy Spirit, in Him we wait, in Him we hope, in Him we trust, in Him we "by love serve one another," and in Him we rejoice saying, singing, praying:

Oh, joy to know that Thou, my Friend,
Art Lord, BEGINNING WITHOUT END,
THE FIRST AND LAST, ETERNAL!
And Thou at length—O glorious grace!
Wilt take me to that holy place,
The home of joys supernal. Amen, Amen!
Come and meet me! Quickly greet me!
With deep yearning, Lord, I look for Thy returning.
Amen.

TLH 343:7

One Chance

The other day I looked at an object
Very carefully.
It was a match. And as I looked
I thought,
"You have ONE CHANCE to light,
ONE CHANCE to do the job you
Were created to do.
If you get wet, or crack,
Or for some reason goof up,
Very likely you will not have your chance to shine."
ONE CHANCE to light,
ONE CHANCE to do the job you were created to do.

It reminds me of my life—ONE CHANCE to live and light the way for future generations. And if my CHANCE escapes, I may not get the CHANCE again, and then I WAS CREATED FOR NOTHING.

John Morrison

Faith and Love

Many people confuse the Scriptural concepts of FAITH AND LOVE. The two, of course, are closely tied together.

For instance, in 1 Corinthians 13:2, Paul says: *"If I have a FAITH that can move mountains, but have not LOVE, I am nothing."*

Because these two Biblical concepts are closely linked, some people get the idea that the two are one and the same—the faith is our love for God, love saves us; that it is love that makes us Christian. Nothing could be farther from the truth of Holy Scripture.

One hears it at some funerals: "She was such a kind and loving person; so good to everyone. Always doing for others." It's as though on that basis God must receive such a person into heaven. However, the Scriptures state most clearly: *"By grace are you saved through faith, and that not of yourselves. It is the gift of God, not of works, lest anyone should boast"* (Eph. 2:8,9).

Though FAITH AND LOVE are closely tied together, they are not the same. Martin Luther expressed the distinction clearly when he wrote: "Faith receives; love gives. Faith brings one to God; love brings him/her to his/her neighbor."

Or to state it another way: Faith leads us from people to God. Love leads us from God to people. That means we, through the power of the Holy Spirit, put our faith (trust), not in ourselves or in other people, but in God. And then, such faith or trust in God compels us to reach out in love to our fellowman.

Faith is simply the hand that receives the free gift of God's grace in Christ Jesus. Clearly, then, faith is not a good work that we perform. It is the trust in the heart created in us by the Holy Spirit. As stated above in Ephesians 2:8, we are saved THROUGH FAITH—not because of our faith.

LOVE, on the other hand, is the fruit or result of FAITH. LOVE to God and to our fellowman is our response to God's free gift of salvation. We do good works and show love to our fellowman—not that we might BECOME people of God, but because we ARE people of God. Truly good works in the sight of God are the fruits of saving faith kindled in our hearts. And to be sure, LOVE TO GOD and to our fellowman is a necessary response or fruit of faith. The Bible states clearly: *"FAITH by itself, if it has no works, is dead"* (James 2:17).

Never, however, dare we think that our love, or the work we do, makes us Christians or that it brings us salvation. We must never confuse cause and effect.

At a funeral let no one try to comfort others by talking about all the supposed good the deceased did. At the time of death there is no other comfort but the Biblical fact that we poor sinners—beggars that we are—are forgiven and declared righteous solely "by grace through faith in Christ Jesus." Oh, yes, "By grace I'm saved, grace free and boundless!"

The second and third verses of ROCK OF AGES state it exactly:

Not the labors of my hands
Can fulfil Thy Law's demands;
Could my zeal no respite know,
Could my tears forever flow,
All for sin could not atone;
THOU MUST SAVE, AND THOU ALONE.

Nothing in my hand I bring,
Simply to Thy cross I cling;
Naked, come to Thee for dress;
Helpless, look to Thee for grace;
Foul, I to the fountain fly,
Wash me, Savior, or I die!

TLH 376:2,3

It is not how much we love, but whether, through the power of the Spirit, we believe and trust in Christ our Savior that determines our relationship with God. Whether we can say and sing from the heart:

I am trusting Thee, Lord Jesus,
Trusting only Thee;
Trusting Thee for full salvation,
Great and free.

TLH 428:1

And where there is such trust, and our relationship with God is right, there will also be LOVE. Remember, true LOVE is the fruit of FAITH. The stronger the FAITH, the greater the LOVE for God and for our fellowman.

FAITH AND LOVE! May the two be inseparable in our hearts and in our lives.

My Maker, strengthen Thou my heart,
O my Redeemer, help impart,
Blest Comforter, keep at my side
That FAITH AND LOVE in me abide.

TLH 541:4

A Plea for Mercy

Recently I was reading about Copernicus. Perhaps to most of us the name Copernicus conjures up the thought of a famed astronomer—a mathematician and scientist. He was that and much more. He was also a man of God who had learned to know and to love and trust Jesus as his Lord and Savior. When he was critically ill and his final moments in this life drew near, he did not think of himself as an astronomer or a scientist or a mathematician; rather, he only thought of himself as a sinner who needed forgiveness of his Lord and Savior. Therefore, he requested that the following epitaph be written on his gravestone:

"Lord, I do not ask the kindness Thou didst show to Peter. I do not dare to ask the grace Thou didst grant to Paul. But, Lord, the MERCY Thou didst show to the dying robber, that MERCY show to me. That earnestly I pray."

That, too, is my foremost plea—A PLEA FOR MERCY. In the several orders of service that we follow in our hymnal, the words MERCY, MERCIES and MERCIFUL are used quite often.

For example, we confess: "O Almighty God, MERCIFUL Father . . . be gracious and MERCIFUL to me, a poor sinful being." We sing: "Lord, have MERCY; Christ have MERCY; Lord, have MERCY." In the Gloria In Excelsis we sing: "O Lord God, Lamb of God, Son of the Father, who takes away the sin of the world, have MERCY on us." In the Prayer of the Church the pastor says: "In peace let us pray to the Lord." The congregation responds: "Lord, have MERCY."

Twice in the Agnus Dei we sing: "O Christ, the Lamb of God, who takes away the sin of the world, have MERCY on us."

In one hundred fifty or so of our hymns we have the words: MERCY, MERCIES and MERCIFUL.

Following are just a few favorites from the Concordance to *The Lutheran Hymnal:*

15:2	17:5	27:2	31:1
33:1	110:2,4	284:1	537:1
545:3	570:1-7	246:1,4	323:1-4
327:1,4	650:2	20:1	39:4
42:4,5	94:1,4	147:1	69:5
187:1	231:1-4	238:4	279:1,4
287:1-12	313:1-3 (2 times in each stanza)		

What a PLEA FOR MERCY! And yet, do you know that in most of the latest versions of the Bible, the word MERCY has been replaced by a variety of words including: pity, gracious, unfailing kindness, etc. All of these are good, salutary words, however, in my humble opinion they don't really wholly embrace what is all included in the word MERCY.

The word MERCY, in a very subtle way, not only tells us something about our wonderful Savior, but also tells us something about ourselves, and reminds us of a dire need that we have; a need for "Grace, MERCY and Peace" which only a loving, gracious, blessed Savior can provide.

David brings this out so beautifully when he prays: "*Have MERCY on me, O God, according to Thy steadfast love; according to Thy abundant MERCY blot out my transgressions. Wash me thoroughly from my iniquity, and cleanse me from my sin*" (Ps. 51:1,2).

Let our past be whatever it has been. Let our sins be "red like crimson" (Isa. 1:18). Let our record be one of repeated failure. Let our conscience clamor with endless accusations. Let our heart be filled with remorse and regret over "*the sin which so easily besets us*" (Heb. 12:1). Let these all be so.

However, praise be to God, we still can pray the pleading prayer of humble Copernicus: "Lord, the MERCY Thou didst show to the dying robber, that MERCY show to me. That earnestly I pray." Whether we realize it or not, the MERCY that was shown the dying thief was the same MERCY that was shown to Peter and Paul, and which is now also available to all who come to the Lord with truly believing and repentant hearts.

And remember, it lies in the very nature of God's abundant grace and MERCY that it is entirely undeserved by us. Peter, Paul, the robber, you and I—we all are dependent on the very same loving kindness and MERCY of our Lord for the full forgiveness of our sins; the unparalleled bounteous love He reveals to us through Calvary's cross.

Let us keep these soul-comforting, strengthening truths in our hearts and minds when we pray THE PRAYER ABOVE ALL PRAYERS—"GOD, be MERCIFUL to me, a sinner."

Shine in our hearts, O Spirit, precious light;
Teach us Jesus Christ to know aright
That we may abide in the Lord who bought us,
Till to our true home he has brought us.
Lord, have MERCY!

LW 155:4

Oh, yes, *"O give thanks unto the Lord, for He is good; for HIS MERCY ENDURES FOR EVER"* (1 Chron. 16:34).

"Surely goodness and MERCY shall follow me all the days of my life; and I will dwell in the house of the Lord for ever." (Ps. 23:6)

Today Thy MERCY calls us
To wash away our sin.
However great our trespass,
Whatever we have been,
However long from MERCY
Our hearts have turned away,
Thy precious blood can cleanse us
And make us white today.

TLH 279:1

Grace, MERCY and peace from God our Father, and from our Lord and Savior, Jesus Christ, be with you all!

SUBJECT: MERCY

In a prayer meeting, a man stood up and prayed, "Lord send justice. All we need is justice. Please give us justice!" Then another man stood up and prayed, "Please don't, Lord! Give us mercy. We need mercy, not justice!"
. . . To which we say "Amen."

Concerning Our Roots

This past year my wife and I have each spent some time genealogizing. In the Greek, *genea* means birth and *logos* means word (discourse). So what we each have been attempting to do is to trace our roots; to trace our family lineage—history.

This interesting, and sometimes intriguing, "science" is often referred to as "tracing our roots," hoping to come up with a genealogical tree that has at least a few good, sound branches. As the window-washer, who slipped from his scaffold and began falling, was heard to say as he passed the 16th floor, "So far, so good!" So it is in tracing our family roots!

Besides a physical lineage, there is also our spiritual heritage—the spiritual family to which we belong since our "rebirth," most often referred to as "the holy Christian Church, the communion of saints." This is certainly a very special family made up solely of believers in the Lord Jesus Christ.

All of which leads me to ask, "How are your *spiritual* roots?" *"As therefore you received Christ Jesus the Lord,"* the Apostle Paul wrote to the Colossians, *"so live in Him, rooted and built up in Him and established in the faith, just as you were taught, abounding in thanksgiving"* (Col. 2:6). And then we read where the Apostle Paul prays for the Ephesians: *"that Christ may dwell in your hearts through faith; that you, being rooted and grounded in love, may know the love of Christ which surpasses knowledge, that you may be filled with all the fullness of God"* (Eph. 3:17).

I was thinking about our "family roots" and also, especially, of our "spiritual roots" as I read about the California redwoods. They are the tallest trees in the world, some rising as high as 300 feet. They are long-standing trees, too, as old as 2500 years!

The detail of interest here is their root system. Most trees have roots that grow as deep as the tree is tall and as wide as its widest branch. Redwood trees, on the other hand, grow in groves with a shallow root system. The roots of one tree intertwine with the roots of other trees surrounding it. The strength of this "locking together" allows the trees to stand tall and long against all kinds of wind and weather. In other words, each tree receives root support from every tree in the grove.

Similarly, we are linked together as Christians by faith in Christ Jesus. And if our faith is alive, strong and healthy, this linkage should provide each of us the strength of every other active Christian rooted in the beautiful, life-granting truths of the precious Word of God. If everything is "good, right and salutary," the intertwining of our faith ought to hold us up together against temptation, suffering and the many different "storms of life" that we experience.

We refer to our spiritual family tree when we confess: "I believe in the Holy Spirit, the holy Christian Church, the communion of saints . . ." Oh, just think of our spiritual family: *"One Lord, one faith, one baptism, one God and Father of us all, who is above all and through all and in all"* (Eph. 4:5,6).

What about our spiritual root system? Like those mighty Redwoods, are our roots strong, healthy and linked together—intertwined, and by love, caring and serving one another?

We must remember who we are and to whom we

belong. Since our baptism we have become members of "the Holy Christian Church, the communion of saints." Paul puts it this way: *"We were all baptized by one Spirit into one body . . . Now you are the body of Christ and each of you is part of it"* (1 Cor. 12:13a, 27). We do not merely belong to the Church, we ARE THE CHURCH! We ARE the Body of Christ! As we so nobly sing:

> Like a mighty army
> Moves the Church of God;
> Brothers, we are treading
> Where the saints have trod.
> We are not divided,
> ALL ONE BODY WE,
> One in hope and doctrine,
> One in charity. . . .

TLH 658:2

The Church must GO, and GLOW and GROW through the Holy Spirit, and it's up to us to make it SO—because WE ARE THE CHURCH.

It is agonizing when Christians fail to support each other in the home—husband and wife, parents and children; and also in the congregation and the church-at-large when there is haughtiness, disregard, pride and arrogance.

Remember our Lord experienced that disregard and neglect in the Garden of Gethsemane. He lamented, "Could you not keep watch with Me for one hour?" The sin of neglect of concern and caring was added to the burden that He took to the cross for all of us.

We are now free to love and support and care fully for one another. He is the strength for all by intertwining with

Christians. Each of us, through the Holy Spirit, must hold fast the support of this "being rooted together" as a high priority value.

There is a section in our hymnals, *The Lutheran Hymnal* and also *Lutheran Worship*, with the heading: THE CHURCH, where the hymns speak especially of the Body of Christ, the Holy Christian Church, the communion of saints, the FAMILY OF GOD. Especially in these hymns we note how we, through the power of the Spirit, have this beautiful oneness in the Lord.

The following hymn is based on these words of the Apostle Paul: *"I . . . beg you to lead a life worthy of the calling to which you have been called, with all lowliness and meekness, with patience, forbearing one another in love, eager to maintain the unity of the Spirit in the bond of peace"* (Eph. 4:1f.). Note the INTERTWINING OF SPIRITUAL ROOTS.

Blest be the tie that binds
Our hearts in Christian love;
The fellowship of kindred minds
Is like to that above.

Before our Father's throne
We pour our ardent prayers;
Our fears, our hopes, our aims, are one,
Our comforts and our cares.

We share our mutual woes,
Our mutual burdens bear,
And often for each other flows
The sympathizing tear.

From sorrow, toil, and pain,
And sin we shall be free
And perfect love and friendship reign
Through all eternity.

TLH 464

Oh, to be like the little boy who was asked by his Sunday school teacher, "Why do you faithfully come to church and Sunday school?" The little guy answered: "I guess it runs in our family; it's in our roots!"

Known But to God

A family from the States decided to take a trip to England. One day their bed and breakfast hosts encouraged them to be sure to include in their schedule a visit to the American cemetery, a short distance from Cambridge, site of one of England's most famous universities.

Established in 1943 on land donated by the University of Cambridge, it is the only permanent World War II military cemetery in the British Isles. The rolling grounds are framed by trees on two sides, and contain 3,811 headstones in seven curved grave plots.

A large number of the service men and women buried there were crew members of British-based American aircraft. Others died in the invasion of North Africa and France, at sea, or in training areas within the United Kingdom.

An impressive "Wall of the Missing" lies alongside a mall with a pool bordered by roses. The wall records names of 5,125 missing in action, lost or buried at sea. Four huge statues represent a soldier, sailor, airman and coast guardsman in uniform.

A mosaic in the chapel of the memorial building stretches across the ceiling above the altar. It depicts the archangel trumpeting the resurrection and the last judgment.

As the visitors of the U.S. walked reverently around the beautiful grounds, they paused at the foot of a grave. It was one of twenty-four decorated with red and white carnations tied with a blue ribbon, and flanked by a tiny American and British flag. The words etched in the headstone read: "Here rests in honored glory a comrade in arms KNOWN BUT TO GOD."

KNOWN BUT TO GOD! These service-people were once known intimately and dearly by fathers, mothers, brothers, sisters, grandparents, friends, perhaps a spouse and children; young men and women who fought for freedom and the dignity of humankind. Yet in death KNOWN BUT TO GOD!

Relatives and friends may forget us, forsake us. We may feel alone in a world that offers many only poverty, cruelty and apathy; but isn't it soul-strengthening to know that the holy Lord God knows each one of us intimately! He knows my sighings and heartaches, my worries and cares. He knows the tears that fall on my pillow at night. He counts them all. *"O Lord, You have searched me and You know me. You know when I sit and when I rise; You perceive my thoughts from afar. You discern my going out and my lying down; You are familiar with all my ways. Before the word is on my tongue you know it completely, O Lord."* (Ps. 139:1-4)

The Lord knows our weaknesses and our strengths. He knows our intentions and our transgressions. The Lord declares: *"For My eyes are upon all their ways; they are not hidden from My face, neither is their iniquity hid from My eyes"* (Jer. 16:17).

In Luke 16:15 we are reminded: *"God knows your hearts."* With the Psalmist we can say: *"When my spirit grows faint within me, it is You, O Lord, who knows my way"* (Ps. 142:3). Oh, yes, *"The ways of man are before the eyes of the Lord, and He ponders all his goings"* (Prov. 5:21).

The Bible states that the Lord is a husband to the widow: *"For your Maker is your husband; the Lord of hosts is His name"* (Isa. 54:5). He is a father to the orphan: *"Father of the fatherless . . . is God in His holy habitation"* (Ps. 68:5).

Isn't it great that, not only are we known to God, but that we know Him; that we are His and He is ours! How we love to sing of this beautiful relationship!

Chief of sinners though I be,
Jesus shed His blood for me;
Died that I might live on high,
Lived that I might never die.
As the branch is to the vine,
I AM HIS, AND HE IS MINE.

TLH 342:1

KNOWN BUT TO GOD! Isn't that the most important relationship of all? Thank God we are known to Him not just in life, not just in death, but for all eternity!

All glory to the Father, Son,
And Holy Spirit, Three in One!
To you, O blessed Trinity,
Be praise throughout ETERNITY! Amen

LW 201:4

God Is

Traveling east on Highway 46 out of Columbus, Indiana, there is a cemetery with a little white sign, on which is printed in black letters: JESUS IS. Whenever I see that little sign I find myself thinking of words and phrases that can readily be added to JESUS IS. For example, JESUS IS Lord, JESUS IS loving, JESUS IS holy, JESUS IS everywhere present at one and the same time, JESUS IS my blessed Savior, JESUS IS God's Son, JESUS IS risen, JESUS IS all-knowing.

The Psalmist does something similar when he declares, *"GOD IS,"* and then he adds, *"OUR REFUGE and STRENGTH, a very present HELP in trouble"* (Ps. 46:1). Let us briefly consider the following three: GOD IS: OUR REFUGE, STRENGTH and HELP.

Usually we think of REFUGE as a shelter, a place of safety, retreat, a stronghold or hiding place.

Have there been times when you felt like running away to hide where no one could ask you questions or tell you what to do or how much you have left undone; where no one could make demands on you or point an accusing finger at your shortcomings? The next time you need a place to hide, a place to be sheltered, try God!

The Psalmist reminds us *"GOD IS OUR REFUGE."* He stands ready to welcome us in His grace and mercy; to purge our penitent hearts with His pardon and peace; to be our mighty Fortress in the hour of temptation; and to embrace us in His arms of love when we have nothing to give except to give up! David reminds us, *"The Lord will be a REFUGE for the oppressed, a REFUGE in times of trouble"* (Ps. 9:9). Again, *"I cried unto You, O Lord; I said, You are my REFUGE and my portion in the land of the living"* (Ps. 142:5). Oh, yes, "Jesus REFUGE of the weary, blest Redeemer, whom we love!" He is, indeed, our "shelter from the stormy blasts."

Are we weak and heavy laden,
Cumbered with a load of care?
Precious Savior, still our REFUGE
Take it to the Lord in prayer.
Do thy friends despise, forsake thee?
Take it to the Lord in prayer;
In His arms He'll take and shield thee,
Thou wilt find a solace there.

TLH 457:3

Not only does the Psalmist declare "GOD IS OUR REFUGE," but he adds, "and STRENGTH." Yes, GOD IS STRENGTH!

Do you ever feel incapable for your tasks, unworthy of the trust placed in you, unable to rise to the level of achievement expected of you? Have you ever felt so tired of trying that you could weep? The next time you feel that way try God!

Remember, our God is STRENGTH! He declares: *"My grace is sufficient for you; for My STRENGTH is made perfect in weakness"* (2 Cor. 12:9). That is why we can join St. Paul in saying: *"When I am weak, then I am strong"* (2 Cor. 12:10). The next time you have a special need for God's STRENGTH, read Psalm 46 or Ephesians 6:10-17. You don't have to "go it alone." With the prophet of old you can confidently declare: *"Behold, God is my salvation; I will trust and not be afraid: for the Lord Jehovah IS MY STRENGTH and my song; He also is become my salvation"* (Isa. 12:2). And may that song of strength and salvation ever be:

Oh, may Thy love inspire my tongue!
SALVATION shall be all my song;
And all my powers shall join to bless
The Lord, my STRENGTH and Righteousness.

TLH 325:6

GOD IS OUR REFUGE, GOD IS OUR STRENGTH. And now the Psalmist adds one more beautiful, soul-comforting and heart-strengthening truth when he declares a third GOD IS, namely, *"GOD IS a very present HELP in trouble"* (Ps. 46:1).

Have you been faced with all kinds of monotonous and multitudinous and trouble-some tasks? Have you run into all kinds of snags and you seem to "strike-out" at every turn? Have you experienced the opposite of what you had expected and hardly know which way to turn or which way to go? Do you feel physically, mentally and spiritually exhausted? Try God!

Even if in all the hurry, scurry, hustle and bustle of life God, at times, seems to be far away and unconcerned, remember: He promises, *"Lo, I AM WITH YOU ALWAYS, even to the end of the age"* (Matt. 28:20). The Bible assures us that *"He is a God at hand and not a God afar off"* (Jer. 23:23).

He is not only our REFUGE and STRENGTH, but the Psalmist assures us that GOD IS *"a very present HELP IN TIME OF TROUBLE"* (Ps. 46:1).

God, our God, does not run away. However, we may! He does not forsake those whom He has redeemed with the blood of His Son—those who put their trust in Him. Though we may not always be aware or mindful of His glorious presence, it is not because He is absent. Our tears, our fears, our worries and our cares may hide His presence from us. Like the Emmaus disciples, we too can have Him walking at our side and not realize His presence. But He is most definitely with us, because He has promised never to leave us or forsake us. He has promised, *"I will never fail you nor forsake you."* Hence we can confidently say, *"The Lord IS MY HELPER, and I will not be afraid"* (Heb. 13:5f.). Let us faithfully heed His ever-open invitation: *"Call upon Me in the day of trouble; I will deliver you, and you shall glorify Me"* (Ps. 50:15).

Our God, our HELP in ages past,
Our HOPE for years to come,
Our SHELTER from the stormy blast,
And our ETERNAL HOME!

TLH 123:1

We need to give God more of a chance to show us who He truly is: Our REFUGE, our STRENGTH and our HELP. He is all of this and much, much more!

O my God, I now commend me
Wholly to Thy mighty hand;
All the powers that Thou dost lend me
Let me use at Thy command.
Lord, my SHIELD,
my STRENGTH divine,
Keep me with Thee - I am THINE. Amen.

TLH 549:6

Only One of Each of Us

Back in the late 1920's and early 1930's, Elsa Surma was the teacher of grades one through three at St. Peter's Lutheran School in North Judson, Indiana. One day as we looked out the windows of our two-room school, large, beautiful snowflakes were softly falling. We children were excited! Perhaps it was the first snow of the season.

I remember our teacher explaining to us that these beautiful, white, lace-like flakes were actually drops of water that, falling through the air, became crystallized as they reached air temperature lower than 32 degrees F. So what we were really seeing were raindrops turned into beautiful, white, countless flakes.

I remember our teacher telling us that no two snow flakes were exactly alike; each one was different. And then she added: "If you think that is amazing, then think of this: there are no two people in all the world who are exactly the same; ONLY ONE OF EACH OF US! *(Following are some thoughts by my mentor, Herman Gockel, that appeared in a church magazine decades ago, entitled, ONLY ONE OF EACH OF US.)*

What a precious, wonderful, soul-comforting thought: ONLY ONE OF EACH OF US. And yet, how seldom we think, let alone ponder this truth! The great and glorious God of heaven and earth who created us and all things—and who guides the sun, the moon and the stars—has ONLY ONE OF EACH OF US, ONE YOU AND ONE ME! In more ways than one we are, indeed, indescribably *"precious in His sight"* (Isa. 43:4).

Again and again the Bible points out that the holy Lord God is deeply concerned about you and about me as individuals—individuals upon whom He is most eager to lavish the fullness of His love and mercy. Perhaps best known are the reassuring words of our blessed Savior when He says: *"Are not two sparrows sold for a penny? And not ONE OF THEM will fall to the ground without your Father's will. But even the hairs of your head are all numbered. Fear not, therefore; YOU ARE OF MORE VALUE than many sparrows"* (Matt. 10:29-31).

And then there are God's very personal words spoken through the prophet Isaiah: *"Behold, I have graven YOU upon the palms of My hands"* (Isa. 49:16). Here we are given the blessed assurance that each of us, you and I, is as close to the Heavenly Father, as dear to Him, as much the object of His daily attention and concern as if our faces had been inscribed on the palms of His omnipotent, loving hands.

Take this to heart, the one and only true God revealed to us through the Holy Scriptures does not only love the world in general, but He knows and loves and cares for EACH ONE OF US INDIVIDUALLY!

"Now thus says the Lord, who created you, . . . Fear not, for I have redeemed you; I have called you by your name, you are Mine" (Isa. 43:1).

We, who through the power of the Holy Spirit have been brought to faith in the Lord Jesus Christ, do not only say, "He died for the sins of all the world," but we also point to Him and say with the Apostle Paul: *"I have been crucified with Christ; it is no longer I who live, but Christ who lives in ME; and the life I now live in the flesh, I live by faith in the Son of God, who loved ME and gave Himself for ME"* (Gal. 2:20). ME, of whom He has ONLY ONE! Remember,

70

ONLY ONE OF EACH OF US! And even though there are billions of people on earth, God dearly cares about YOU and He cares about me.

Keeping that very special beautiful truth in mind, see what effect it has on you as you read the following Psalms emphasizing the pronouns: I, my and me (23, 25, 27, 51, 57, 73 and all your other favorites).

Down Here for Up There

During the Great Depression of the thirties a good man lost his job, exhausted his savings and forfeited his house. His grief was multiplied by the sudden death of his precious wife. The only thing he had left was his faith, and it was weakening.

One day he was combing the neighborhood looking for work. He stopped to watch some men who were doing the stonework on a church building. One of those men was skillfully chiseling a triangular piece of stone. Not seeing a spot where it would fit, he asked, "Where are you going to put that?" The man replied, "See that little opening up there near the spire? That's where it goes. I'M SHAPING IT DOWN HERE SO IT WILL FIT UP THERE."

Tears filled the down-trodden man's eyes as he walked away. He had learned an important lesson through these words: "SHAPING IT DOWN HERE SO IT WILL FIT IN UP THERE." He found new meaning in his difficult situation.

Perhaps some of you are going through troublesome times. You may be experiencing some heartbreaking sorrow. Or perhaps you are enduring some painful physical illness. Or maybe it is a family problem that is causing anxiety in your heart and mind. Or it may well be something else; something that may be too painful to talk to anyone else about. The blows of the hammer and chisel often do hurt and the pain can be excruciating.

However, in the power and strength of the Holy Spirit, hold on to your faith in the Lord Jesus Christ. By trusting in the Lord you will discover that these difficulties won't get you down. Remember, they are only temporary. With that kind of faith the Apostle Paul was able to write, *"I consider that the sufferings of this present time are not worth comparing with the glory that is to be revealed to us"* (Rom. 8:18).

The holy Lord God bids us: *"Call upon Me in the day of trouble, I will deliver you, and you shall glorify Me"* (Ps. 50:15). He promises, *"I am with you, and will keep you in all places"* (Gen. 28:15). He lovingly reminds us: *"In the world you shall have tribulations, but be of good cheer; I have overcome the world"* (John 16:33).

In order to comfort his mother in a time of great sorrow, Joseph Scriven, about 1855, wrote the following:

What a Friend we have in Jesus,
All our sins and griefs to bear!
What a privilege to carry
Ev'rything to God in prayer!
Oh, what peace we often forfeit,
Oh, what needless pain we bear,
All because we do not carry
Ev'rything to God in prayer!

Have we trials and temptations?
Is there trouble anywhere?
We should never be discouraged,
Take it to the Lord in prayer.
Can we find a Friend so faithful
Who will all our sorrows share?
Jesus knows our ev'ry weakness—
Take it to the Lord in prayer.

Are we weak and heavy laden,
Cumbered with a load of care?
Precious Savior, still our Refuge—
Take it to the Lord in prayer.
Do thy friends despise, forsake thee?
Take it to the Lord in prayer;
In His arms He'll take and shield thee,
Thou wilt find a solace there. Amen.

TLH 457

Hands

A pastor went to a funeral home to pay his respects to an old acquaintance and good friend. Some thoughtful person had placed a well-worn Bible in the hands of the departed. It looked fitting and symbolic.

The pastor could well recall how her face would glow with radiance of one of God's faithful ones as she studied the Word in Bible class. On his visits to her he would find her ready to read and talk the Word with her pastor. Yes, it was fitting to have God's Word in her hands even on this occasion.

Later the pastor thought: What if someone put that which seemed most appropriate in my hands after my soul took leave of this world—what would it be? Would it be a cigarette? A golf club? A fishing rod? A tennis racquet? A set of car keys? A TV channel selector? A deck of cards? A football? A worn Bible? A Bible not worn at all? A thought: What would be the most appropriate thing in YOUR HANDS?

Hands

A good marriage is a lifetime of hands.
It's a shaking hand sliding a shiny gold band onto the
    finger of another shaking hand.
It's an anxious hand tugging on a suddenly shy hand.
It's a calm hand holding an apprehensive hand.
It's two ecstatic hands being grasped by
        tiny new hands.
It's hands touching in sudden tenderness and love.
It's a big and a little hand clasped that somehow
    always just fit.
It's an optimistic hand patting a discouraged hand.
It's a panicky hand clutching a more calm hand.
It's a tense, rigid hand touching a disturbed,
    trembling hand.
It's busy hands reaching out to serve other hands.
It's waving hands from the windows of a car
    that's leaving.
It's expressive hands beckoning, "Help me, please!"
It's tender hands sharing sadness with a touch.
It's concerned hands holding fevered hands.
It's a thankful hand holding another thankful hand
    during the sermon in church.
It's folded hands joining in humble, fervent prayer.
It's hands of faith receiving the joys at God's
    right hand.
It's a mournful hand sliding a dull gold band
    off the finger of a very still hand.

It's a wrinkled hand still pointing others to Jesus,
the Way, the Truth and the Life.
Finally, it's a waiting hand lovingly clasped by the
blessed Savior and taken home to join those who
have gone before.

*"Into Thy hand I commit my spirit; Thou hast redeemed
me, O Lord, faithful God."*

(Ps. 31:5)

God's Hand

Father so gently, oh take my hand,
Deep are the waters, I know not the way;
Sleepless the nights, confused is the day;
All is so empty, so lone do I stand.

God, I believe, but the burden is sore,
Faith and fresh courage are all I implore.
Give calm to my heart, that will banish all fear,
Open my eyes, that Your purpose may be clear,

Answer my wonder, dispel all my doubt.
Teach me the lesson of doing without;
Tho' hard be the cross, with help I can stand,
Father so gentle, I reach out my hand.

Hearken, My child, believe in My Word,
Surrender yourself to Me; I am your Lord;
Earth's deepest sorrows they last but a day;
Fresh courage I will give you: I am the Way.

Look up and trust; for the sun shines on high,
No shadow lies there; clear blue is the sky.
On guard are the stars, bringing calm to your sleep;
Learn peace: have faith that your watch I will keep.

Dry now your tears, make your heart bright with cheer,
Grief cannot blind you, your way I make clear;
Have faith; I am near, at your side do I stand.
I am your Guide; put your trust in My hand.

Hands

There are hands that help and comfort
Hands that plan and teach
Hands that rest and hands that strive
For a goal just out of reach . . .

Hands that grasp and hands that give
Hands that work and play
Friendly hands and loving hands
That soothe life's cares away

But praying hands are dearest
In the sight of God above
For in their sweet and earnest clasp
Is reverence and love . . .

No hands can do an unkind act
Nor cause another care
Nor sin against our Father's love
When they are clasped in prayer.

My Jesus, as You will; Oh, may Your will be mine!
Into YOUR HAND OF LOVE I would my all resign.
Thro' sorrow or thro' joy conduct me as Your own
And help me still to say, my Lord, Your will be done.
                                        Amen.

Not "I Think," "I Feel," "It Seems to Me," But Rather, "I Know" and "I Am Persuaded"

The other day I was examining some Bible study booklets. I was somewhat surprised and disappointed how often two questions appeared and reappeared in the various lessons, namely, "What do you think?" and "How do you feel?"

I was reminded of a story that goes something like this: A young pastor had just completed what he thought was a brilliant sermon. Descending from the pulpit, he entered the sacristy with a confident and lively step.

There followed a moment of uncomfortable silence as he awaited some word of comment from the veteran clergyman seated thoughtfully in a chair.

Finally the young man ventured uncertainly: "Well, what did you think of the sermon?" The older man replied in a tone which was friendly but very serious. "Young man," he said, "your sermons are too seem-y. Do you realize that more than a dozen times you said: 'It seems to me . . .' Those people out there didn't come to church this morning to hear how things seemed to you. They wanted to know how things appear to God—above all, how they appear to Him. They wanted to hear a straightforward, unequivocal 'Thus saith the Lord!' Not what you think, how you feel, what it seems to you or your opinions, but what He says—His Word!"

The older man was right. What the world needs today is more people, men, women and children, of courage and conviction, who will take their stand with the Apostle Paul and say: *"I know whom I have believed, and am persuaded that He is able to keep that which I have committed unto Him against that day" (2 Tim. 1:12)*. Or with the Apostle John, who said: *"That which we have seen and heard declare we to you" (1 John 1:3)*.

If there is a phrase that would sound incongruous on the lips of Christ's apostles after the great miracle of Pentecost, it is the phrase, "it seems to me."

To the early Christians it didn't seem that Christ was the promised Messiah of the Hebrews; that He had risen victorious from the tomb; that He had appeared to upwards of 500; that He had ascended visibly and triumphantly into heaven; that He would return again in glory. These things they knew! Of these things they were certain! And these things they proclaimed—at the risk of their very lives.

In a day of spreading doubt and unbelief, we dare not settle for a *seem-y* religion—a religion of maybes and perhapses—a religion based on what others think or how they feel. Such is not the faith our blessed Savior left us. Such is not the faith His followers preached. He knew—and they knew—that His glorious Gospel was and is the THE TRUTH (John 14:6).

May we, guided and strengthened by the Holy Spirit, faithfully and diligently search the Scriptures that we might come to lay hold of the unquestioning and undaunted faith of the great apostle who exclaimed: *"I know whom I have believed" (2 Tim. 1:12)*. And *"I am persuaded that neither death nor life nor angels nor principalities nor powers nor things present nor things to come, nor height nor depth nor any other creature shall be able to separate us from the love of God, which is in Christ Jesus our Lord" (Rom. 8:38-39).*

St. Paul's was not a religion of "I think," "I feel" or "It seems to me." His was a religion of "I KNOW!" So it must be with us.

I KNOW my faith is founded
On Jesus Christ, my God and Lord;
And this my faith confessing,
Unmoved I stand on his sure Word.
Man's reason cannot fathom
The truth of God profound;
Who trusts its subtle wisdom
Relies on shifting ground.
GOD'S WORD IS ALL SUFFICIENT,
It makes divinely sure,
And trusting in its wisdom,
My faith shall rest secure.

LW 354:1

"Stop wrestling with God's Word and start resting on it."

A Vision of Jesus

The following incident is said to have happened in the church of a well-known clergyman.

He was a popular man, eloquent in speech, a great orator. He held the attention of the people. Church attendance had gone up. He received a lot of accolades. One Monday morning, however, he found a slip of paper placed in his Bible by some member of his congregation with these words written upon it: "We would see Jesus."

The pastor was distressed, but being honestly desirous of being a shepherd, not a hireling, he was not offended, but endeavored to examine himself and his work humbly and sincerely. He carefully went over the sermons that he had preached and he discovered that, for the most part, he was not preaching Christ. The Lord Jesus and His Word and work, to a great extent, were missing in his sermons. God's plan of salvation for all mankind was not being heralded by him. Confession, repentance, absolution and witnessing were not being stressed.

After much prayer, examination, perspiration and determination, the pastor now faithfully heralded Christ as Savior and Lord, and within a short time another slip of paper was placed in the Bible on the pulpit with the following words: "Then were the disciples glad, when they saw the Lord."

Our Seminary class motto in 1947 was:
"Preach the Word . . . in season and out of season"

(2 Tim. 4:2).

The Same, But Different

This morning our local paper carried an article about a Butterfly Ranch in Putnam County, Indiana. Recently an elementary school summer outdoor science class visited the Butterfly Ranch to learn, first hand, how a butterfly develops from the lowly caterpillar to a chrysalis in its cocoon.Then through an amazing metamorphosis it becomes the beautiful butterfly. It is now able to fly over the walls which it could not crawl over before. It is an entirely different creature, and yet, it is still the same creature. THE SAME, BUT DIFFERENT!

After the butterfly life-cycle demonstration, the children were allowed to go inside a mesh cage to see the butterflies close at hand as they would light on the children. The visiting class was then taught the finer points of netting a butterfly—after which the children were each given a net as they eagerly went to the meadow to catch the prettiest one on the ranch.

For many people one of the most exciting and beautiful Easter symbols is the colorful butterfly. Why the butterfly? Because of the transformation that it represents—from a lowly caterpillar to a chrysalis in its cocoon to the beautiful butterfly.

This is how it is with the Resurrection of our Lord Jesus Christ. He is no longer bound by time or by space to which He willingly bound Himself for our sakes. His bruised and bleeding Body is now glorified and He comes to His hiding, frightened disciples through locked doors. He is already there, for the exaltation of His human nature has already taken place. His nail-scarred hands and feet now carry scars that are glorified!

The resurrected Christ appears and vanishes. He is still the same Lord whom the apostles knew before, but He is different! The butterfly reminds us of that. THE SAME, BUT DIFFERENT! He is God and He is Man. As God and Man He reigns over all things for the good of His people, "the Holy Christian Church, the Communion of Saints."

The butterfly is also a symbol of our resurrection as children of God in Christ Jesus. In the Apostles' Creed we keep saying, "I believe in the Resurrection of the body!" Why, yes! Your body! My body! This is Jesus' promise, "Because I live, you shall live also." St. Paul says in Philippians 3:21: *"(Christ) will transform our lowly bodies so that they will be like His glorious body."* THE SAME, BUT DIFFERENT! What happened to Jesus in His Resurrection will happen to us in our resurrection. In our resurrection we will be THE SAME, BUT DIFFERENT— like the butterfly!

Here are the words spoken at the grave regarding the body: *"It is sown in corruption; it is raised in glory. It is sown in weakness; it is raised in power. It is sown a natural body; it is raised a spiritual body . . . So when this corruptible shall have put on incorruption, and this mortal shall have put on immortality, then shall be brought to pass the saying that is written, Death is swallowed up in victory. O Death, where is thy sting? O Grave, where is thy victory? The sting of death is sin; and the strength of sin is the Law. But thanks be to God, which giveth us the victory through our Lord Jesus Christ"* (1 Cor. 15:53-57).

On the day of resurrection our bodies will rise. These same bodies we have now will rise and be with Christ. I will be me. You will be you. We will be the same persons we are now, but we will be different! Like Christ! Like the butterfly! THE SAME, BUT DIFFERENT! In his first epistle St. John writes, *"Beloved, we are God's children now; it does not yet appear what we shall be, but we know that when He appears we shall be like Him, for we shall see Him as He is" (1 John 3:2).*

THE SAME, BUT DIFFERENT! All this is true because Christ's death has transformed our death. He took our sin and rebellion as His own and died the death of God's curse for us. Then He rose from the dead and by that Resurrection defeated death FOR US!

As we each Sunday, the first day of the week, celebrate Christ's glorious Resurrection, we rejoice with joy unspeakable, for we know that one day, together with our resurrected Lord and Master, we too, in the eternal home, will be still THE SAME, BUT DIFFERENT!

I know that my Redeemer lives;
What comfort this sweet sentence gives!
He lives, He lives, who once was dead;
He lives, my ever-living Head.

He lives triumphant from the grave,
He lives eternally to save,
He lives all-glorious in the sky,
He lives exalted there on high.

He lives to bless me with His love,
He lives to plead for me above,
He lives my hungry soul to feed,
He lives to help in time of need.

He lives to silence all my fears,
He lives to wipe away my tears,
He lives to calm my troubled heart,
He lives all blessings to impart.

He lives and grants me daily breath;
He lives, and I shall conquer death;
He lives my mansion to prepare;
He lives to bring me safely there.

He lives, all glory to His name!
He lives, my Jesus, still the same.
Oh, the sweet joy this sentence gives,
"I know that my Redeemer lives!" Amen.

TLH 200

An Anchor That Holds

For many years a fisherman had worked hard and saved his money. Finally he was able to buy his own 40-foot fishing vessel which he named Red Fish. He was single and reveled in his life alone upon the water. He enjoyed being his own boss and was happy to be free from many worries and responsibilities which other people have. He said: "Don't let anyone tell you that a fisherman doing his own thing, and being his own boss, doesn't have a good life, because it is!"

However, his "good life on his own" came to an abrupt end through a failure on his part. He left San Pedro, California, at 9 p.m. one night and reached his destination off Catalina Island about 3 a.m. the next morning. It was raining and cold, so he thought he would get a couple hours of sleep before beginning his morning of fishing; but HE FAILED TO DROP ANCHOR! He locked his cabin ports and turned on his propane stove to keep warm.

The next thing he knew he had drifted ashore and was on the rocks with several large holes into the hull of his boat. He managed to send out an S.O.S. before he fell unconscious from the diesel fumes. The coast guard received his message and was able to make a hazardous but heroic rescue of the fisherman—though his boat was a total wreck.

Many people today are busy "doing their own thing." They have not reckoned with the STORMS ON THE SEA OF LIFE. They are drifting without an anchor for their souls. And without a spiritual anchor, they will find themselves on the rocks and apart from a spiritual rescue, they will perish.

Are we prepared for "the storms of life"? Do we have an anchor that holds? The Psalmist cries out to the Lord: *"Deep calls to deep at the thunder of Your waterfalls; all Your waves and Your breakers have gone over me" (Ps. 42:7).* And again, *"Your wrath lies heavy on me, and You have overwhelmed me with Your waves" (Ps. 88:7).*

How very grateful we must be that there is a sure and safe anchor on which we can depend. In Hebrews 6:19f. we read: *"We have this as a sure and steadfast ANCHOR OF THE SOUL, a hope that enters into the inner shrine behind the curtain, where Jesus has gone as a forerunner on our behalf."*

Just as the anchor of a ship holds the vessel safe and secure, even against strong winds and dangerous waves, thus the hope of our faith, being anchored in the promises of the Lord Jesus Christ, gives us a firm and safe hold on salvation in the midst of all storms and tempests. This anchor of our soul, by the grace of God, is firmly imbedded in the very presence of Almighty God, in the most holy place of the heavens, where Jesus, God's own Son and our Savior, has entered to become our Advocate with the Father, to intercede for us with a continual reference to His perfect work of atonement in our behalf. It is Jesus in whom we believe, in whom we firmly trust, in whom our salvation has been secured, and in whom our hope of salvation rests, ANCHORED in the Almighty God Himself.

The Lord Jesus left heaven's glory and came to earth. For our sakes He let the billows of God's judgment roll over Him. But on the third day He arose again from the grave and now in the heavenly harbor is waiting to receive all who, through the power of the Holy Spirit, put their trust in Him.

Is He the anchor of your soul? Is He the HOPE of your salvation? Remember, the symbol for HOPE IS THE ANCHOR. (There is a saying, "Hope is oxygen for the soul.")

We can joyfully, thankfully sing with all the redeemed:

My HOPE is built on nothing less
Than Jesus' blood and righteousness;
I dare not trust the sweetest frame,
But wholly lean on Jesus' name.
On Christ, the solid Rock, I stand;
All other ground is sinking sand.

When darkness veils His lovely face,
I rest on His unchanging grace;
IN EV'RY HIGH AND STORMY GALE
MY ANCHOR HOLDS WITHIN THE VEIL.
On Christ, the solid Rock, I stand;
All other ground is sinking sand.

His oath, His covenant, and blood
Support me in THE WHELMING FLOOD;
When ev'ry earthly prop gives way,
He then is all my HOPE and STAY.
On Christ, the solid Rock, I stand
All other ground is sinking sand.

When He shall come with trumpet sound,
Oh, may I then in Him be found,
Clothed in His righteousness alone,
Faultless to stand before the throne.
On Christ, the solid Rock, I stand;
All other ground is sinking sand. Amen.

TLH 370

Oh, yes, we have AN ANCHOR that keeps the soul steadfast and sure while the billows roll, fastened to the Rock which cannot move, grounded firm and deep in the Savior's love.

If on earth my days He lengthen,
He my weary soul will strengthen;
All my trust in Him I place.
Earthly wealth is now abiding,
Like a stream away is gliding;
SAFE I ANCHOR IN HIS GRACE.

TLH 425:6

When our lives become stormy, when we are blown off course and we lose our bearings, it is good to remember that we have a incomparable Navigational Guide in the Bible, and an incomparable Pilot in the Lord Jesus Christ who knows the way, and in fact, HE IS THE WAY!

Church Broken Into

One night a certain church had been broken into. The safe had been pried open and the contents ransacked and scattered all over the basement of the church. A tape recorder and a Bell & Howell projector had also been stolen from the premises.

Not only was the break-in immediately reported to the police, but new and more modern locks were installed and other security measures were taken. The membership was instructed to make certain that all doors and windows were secured before leaving the premises.

The break-in was reported in the congregation's monthly NEWSLETTER, and everyone was alerted to be mindful of a rash of church break-ins taking place in the neighborhood.

Not long after that, the church was broken into again and generally ransacked. The cross on the altar, a large lectern Bible and the Communion ware were stolen. Also a swivel chair and a number of other things were taken from the premises by the thieves.

This break-in was also reported to the law enforcement agency. It was a big loss, and how anyone would have the audacity to steal these things from the church seemed to be beyond comprehension. Again, more safety measures were put into place and again, through the monthly church NEWSLETTER, the congregation was notified of the loss and everyone was talking about the church break-ins.

Several weeks later the monthly NEWSLETTER was sent to the homes in the congregation with the headlines repeated: CHURCH BROKEN INTO! HELP!! THIEF!!!

The article went on to say that the thief had been at work for some time and had done considerable damage. WHAT WAS STOLEN? Over half of the members missing from worship every Sunday except on Easter. Many girls and boys missing from Sunday school, and even more adults missing from Bible class. The article further stated that the offerings and pledges of many members were missing; and many have been robbed of the joy of worshipping and working together with their fellow-members. Oh, yes, a lot of stealing going on in the church!

Who is the thief? The NEWSLETTER reported: By the evidence he has left, we have determined his identity as the devil, the world and sinful flesh (usually referred to as the unholy trinity). The NEWSLETTER stated: This criminal has stolen a portion of our spiritual power—deprived our Heavenly Father of worship and praise—stolen many precious lambs from the flock of the Good Shepherd—and looted the Lord's treasury.

How does the thief operate? HE STARTS IN THE HOMES OF THE MEMBERS OF THE CONGREGATION. He offers them many excuses for not worshipping. He convinces them that other things are more important than precious time with the Lord and fellow-members of the household of faith. The article went on to state: The thief steals loyalty to God, faithfulness in worship, steadfastness of service, joy in giving, and love for the Lord Jesus Christ who laid down His life for all mankind.

The congregation was warned: "Beware of this thief! He works slyly and cunningly. He may be lurking nearby determined to steal more precious blood-bought souls. No insurance company covers the damage he does. No law enforcement can keep him captive. So beware that the thief and robber doesn't break in on you and your loved ones.

"What can you do to keep this thief away? Recall, again, what the blessed Savior has done for you; what His love for you demanded of Him. Think about the precious blessings of forgiveness and the assurance of eternal life that the thief is endeavoring to steal from you and your loved ones. Resolve right here and now, together with your family, to take time out for the Lord in worship, in prayer, in private and family devotions, in sharing the fellowship of the members of the family of faith. No question about it, this takes a lot of discipline and determination, but in the strength of the Lord it is possible, and you will never, ever have regrets.

"Therefore, for the sake of precious blood-bought souls, in the love and strength of the Lord, all of our members are encouraged to make the following their heart-felt determination and resolve to stop the soul-stealing thief:"

Then here will I and mine today
A solemn cov'nant make and say:
Though all the world forsake his Word,
My house and I will serve the Lord.

LW 467:4

Our Family

God brought us together.

We need one another,
We love one another,
We forgive one another,
We work together,
We play together,
We worship together.

Together we use God's Word . . .
Together we grow in Christ . . .
Together we love all people . . .
Together we serve our God . . .
Together we hope for heaven . . .
Through Christ, our Lord!

These are our hopes and ideals.

Help us to attain them, O God.

One of the best things parents can leave their children are happy, God-blessed memories.

Sow the Seed

About seven years ago Jeff VanOsdol, a member of Faith congregation, was about ready to leave on his VICARAGE. He wrote an article for our monthly Newsletter on the subject of VICARAGE. Jeff, who is now a pastor in Cupertino, California, wrote: "A Vicarage is similar to the internships served in many other educational programs. I will be assigned to a parish somewhere in the United States, and Jennie and I will move there and for one year I will serve as the Vicar of the church. The duties performed by the Vicar vary from congregation to congregation, but usually include experiences in several pastoral activities: preaching, teaching, making nursing home and hospital visits, learning how a congregation functions, and just generally 'tagging along' with the pastor, always observing."

Having now served in the parish ministry for several years I am quite certain that Jeff would expand the list of activities performed by a vicar and a pastor. However, I believe that everything required and expected of a vicar and a pastor could be summed up in one, short phrase, only three little words: SOW THE SEED! That's it, SOW THE SEED OF GOD'S WORD!

It almost appears to be an over-simplification to say that this is all a pastor and vicar need to do. And it almost seems to be a little humiliating—after earning all those credit hours and degrees at a number of different colleges, universities and the Seminary—and then to say your one task is to SOW THE SEED, THE SEED OF

GOD'S WORD. And yet, that really covers it. SOW THE SEED! In preaching, teaching and in every type of counseling—the SEED MUST BE SOWN. In all church organizations, in all meetings of boards and committees for whatever purpose, the SEED OF GOD'S WORD must be sown. When promoting evangelism, stewardship and education, in the strength of the Lord the pastor must SOW THE SEED! In all his calls, visits and writings, the SEED MUST BE SOWN.

Sow It Faithfully

Add nothing to it. Subtract nothing from it. Do not question it. Do not debate it. In the power of the Spirit search it, believe it, embrace it, share it. SOW THE SEED!

Sow It Expectantly

It is good Seed. Its power will amaze you because all the power, light and life and love of God is in it. It will produce. It will not return void. It's all you have. It's all you need. SOW THE SEED!

Sow It Patiently

Remember, some of the Seed will fall on very hard ground. There is a lot of hostility out there in the world. Other Seed will fall among the thistles and thorns and will be smothered. Some will sprout and grow for a while and then die. It will cause your heart to ache when that happens. But you can't quit. SOW THE SEED! Some will fall on good heart soil and bring forth and bear abundant fruit.

If pastors would be faithful to the Lord and to those entrusted to their spiritual care and keeping, they must faithfully, diligently, lovingly SOW THE SEED. There may well be other things that they will do, but this is the one thing they must continue faithfully to do—SOW THE SEED of God's holy, inerrant, sacred, saving Word. SOW THE SEED and keep sowing—that is Jesus' message to us! Let me be a sower, Lord, and leave the growing to You!

Almighty God, Thy Word is cast
Like seed into the ground;
Now let the dew of heav'n descend
And righteous fruits abound.

Oft as the precious seed is sown,
Thy quickening grace bestow
That all whose souls the truth receive
Its saving power may know. Amen.

TLH 49:1,4

Here Thy praise is gladly chanted,
Here Thy seed is duly sown;
Let my soul, where it is planted,
Bring forth precious sheaves alone,
So that all I hear may be
Fruitful unto life in me.

TLH 1:3

A Most Profound Thought

The renowned theologian Dr. Karl Barth was spending an evening within the intimate circle of friends. Curious to know more about the great theologian's thinking, one of those present asked him: "What is the most profound thought that ever entered your mind?"

After a brief moment of reflection, Dr. Barth replied very simply: "The most profound thought I have ever known is the simple truth: *'Jesus loves me, this I know, for the Bible tells me so.'*"

About Sermon Writing

Labor and toil—it takes that. It takes selective reading and ever more reading. It takes writing and endless rewriting. It takes thinking by day and some tossing on your bed at night.

It takes an insatiable dissatisfaction with your best efforts and merciless cutting out of everything—word, phrase, paragraph and even sermon—that does not supremely serve the one glorious purpose of a sermon, namely, to touch, move, guide, comfort, strengthen and inspire hearts through the power of the Holy Spirit—to believe, react, share and dearly to love God and our fellowman with heart and hands and voices.

And the greatest compliment a pastor can receive on his sermon: "Oh, pastor, what a great, merciful, wonderful, loving Lord and Savior Jesus Christ we have!"

"Fleiszig gebeten ist ueber die Haelfte getan."
(Diligent prayer is over half of the work.)
— Martin Luther

John Wesley was once asked what he would do if he learned that this was to be his last day on earth.

Without hesitation he enumerated the things of his daily routine: Bible study, prayer, visiting the sick and preaching.

What About the Title, "Vicar"?

In the preceding meditation we wrote about a young man from our congregation who was about to leave on his VICARAGE. Presently another young man from our congregation is serving as a VICAR in the Cleveland, Ohio, area.

Next fall another man from our congregation will be leaving the Seminary to serve a year of VICARAGE, and presently we have a VICAR serving in our congregation. All of which brings up the question, WHAT ABOUT THE NAME OR TITLE, "VICAR"?

If you would look up the word VICAR in a dictionary you would note such words as: a substitute, a deputy, an assistant, one acting on behalf or representing another, taking the place of another.

Now, what about the name or title "Vicar"? When we study the Scriptures in Confirmation class and otherwise, we read and speak of the VICARIOUS ATONEMENT. (Check page 114 in the old Catechism or page 133 in the new edition.) VICARious comes from the word, VICAR, which has the root meaning of "substitute." CHRIST JESUS was our Substitute, our VICAR. He took our place under God's judgment against sin. By paying the penalty of our guilt through His suffering and death on the cross, Christ, our VICAR, atoned, or made satisfaction, for our sins. In Isaiah 54:3f. we are assured: "Surely He (Christ Jesus, our Lord) bore OUR infirmities and carried OUR sorrows, yet we considered Him stricken by God, smitten by Him and afflicted. But He was pierced for OUR transgressions, He was crushed for OUR iniquities; the punishment that brought US peace was upon HIM, and by HIS wounds WE ARE HEALED." That is VICARious ATONEment.

To ATONE means to reconcile; to make satisfaction. That great theologian, the Apostle Paul, writes: "We also rejoice in God through our Lord Jesus Christ, THROUGH WHOM WE HAVE RECEIVED RECONCILIATION" (Rom. 5:11). ATONEMENT is the act of making amends or making satisfaction so that those who have been separated from God by sin might be brought together and be AT ONE with Him; that we might have ATONEMENT or AT-ONE-MENT with Christ, our blessed Lord and Savior. In 1 John 2:2 we are assured, *"He is the ATONING sacrifice for OUR sins, and not only for OURS but also for the sins of the whole world."* And in 1 John 4:10 we are reminded: *"This is love; not that we loved God, but that He loved us and sent His Son as an ATONING sacrifice for our sins."* And this, as we well know, He fully accomplished through His suffering and death, and through His glorious resurrection and ascension.

Therefore we joyfully, thankfully say and sing:

Since Christ has full ATONEMENT made
And brought to us salvation,
Each Christian therefore may be glad
And build on this foundation.
Your grace alone, dear Lord, I plead,
Your death is now my life indeed,
For you have paid my ransom.

LW 355:4

In Christ Jesus we have the ultimate VICAR! What a grand and meaningful title for a young man serving the Lord and His people!

He Was All Paid Up

An elderly Christian gentleman was at the point of death. The attending physician gathered sufficient courage to whisper, "Sir, it appears that you do not have long to live. If you have any accounts to settle, you had better settle them now."

The old man replied weakly but confidently: "I have no accounts to settle. I took care of my debts to my fellowmen as they came due, and my Lord and Savior has paid all my debts to God in full!"

He was right. Christ Jesus has paid the debt of every member of the human family. Clearly and emphatically the Bible declares: *"For God so loved the world that He gave His only Son, that whoever believes in Him may have eternal life" (John 3:16).* When Christ died on the cross at Calvary, He paid the penalty of every sin of all mankind.

That is what the Bible means when it says: *"Christ the Lord bore our sins in His body on the tree, that we might die to sin and live to righteousness. By His wounds you have been healed" (1 Peter 2:24).*

And what is left for us to do? Believe it with all our heart! The dying man found no comfort in the fact that he had lived a good life. His only comfort lay in the fact that "my Savior has paid all my debts to God." By grace through faith he believed it, and by believing he shared in the release which Christ had purchased. Through Christ the Lord, and through Him alone, HE WAS ALL PAID UP!

Through Christ we, too, ARE ALL PAID UP! The Bible says, *"God was in Christ, reconciling the world unto Himself, not imputing their trespasses unto them"*—that is, *not charging our sins to our account* (2 Cor. 5:19).

At the foot of the Cross on Calvary lies the handwriting that once stood against us but is now blotted out, its accusations forever covered by the atoning blood of Jesus. And from heaven comes the divine acknowledgment; the receipt which God Himself has sealed forever by the glorious resurrection of His dear Son: PAID IN FULL! Freely, forever forgiven through the Savior's precious blood and His innocent suffering and death.

Therefore, through the power of the Holy Spirit, let us confess, repent, believe and spread the glorious, sacred, saving Gospel as we lift our hearts and voices:

He blotted out with His own blood
The judgment that against us stood;
He full atonement for us made,
AND ALL OUR DEBT HE FULLY PAID.

TLH 163:2

Are You Born Again?

Several years ago a Minneapolis, Minnesota, newspaper poll stated that 20% of Minnesotans had a "born again experience." The poll pointed out that this figure was approximately half the national average.

On the basis of the Holy Scriptures we must say that if a person, through the power of the Holy Spirit, is a professing Christian, that person HAS BEEN BORN AGAIN! Very clearly Jesus stated: "Except one is born again, he cannot see the kingdom of God . . . Except one is born of water and of the Spirit, he cannot enter into the kingdom of God." (John 3:3,5)

The Apostle Paul referred to being "born again" as "regeneration" when he, by divine inspiration, wrote: "When the goodness and loving kindness of God our Savior appeared, He saved us, not because of deeds done by us in righteousness, but in virtue of His own mercy, by the washing of regeneration and renewal in the Holy Spirit, which He poured out upon us richly through Jesus Christ our Savior, so that we might be justified by His grace and become heirs in hope of eternal life" (John 3:3-7).

ARE YOU BORN AGAIN? A child of God can say emphatically: "Yes!" Either this occurred at baptism or it came about as a result of hearing the Gospel message of salvation. The Holy Spirit worked a miracle in your heart through the power of the means of grace (Word and Sacraments).

However, when people talk about "a born again

EXPERIENCE," they usually emphasize "experience"-saying that you can only be certain of being a Christian if you have had some type of memorable emotional experience.

No one can deny that some people have such vivid experiences and can point to a precise time when they were converted or born again. However, when it is stated that a person cannot be a Christian unless they have had such an emotional experience, that is definitely not stated in the Scriptures and must, therefore, be rejected. If that were really the case we would base the hope and certainty of our salvation on our feelings.

We are saved, not because we feel saved. Feelings are not dependable—they constantly change. Rather, we are saved solely because Jesus Christ has redeemed us and promised that all who trust in Him for forgiveness and life will be saved. "Nobody can always have devout feelings; and even if we could, feelings are not what God principally cares about . . . Feelings come and go, His love for us continues." (C. S. Lewis)

This very important truth is underscored by two lines in a chorale—"I cling to what my Savior taught and trust it, whether felt or not."

Through the power of the Holy Spirit we trust the word and promises of God. They, unlike our feelings, do not change. Our Lord remains faithful. Even in our darkest days when we may feel that God deserted us, we can, on the basis of His promises, say: "I know Whom I have believed and am persuaded that He is able to keep that which I have committed unto Him against that day" (2 Tim. 1:12).

That beautiful, soul-comforting passage, by the way was the favorite Bible verse of a dear lady. How often she would repeat that Word of the Lord! Everyone who called on her in the nursing home and later on her death bed, heard from her lips that heart-felt confession: "I know Whom I have believed and am persuaded that He is able to keep that which I have committed unto Him against that day" (2 Tim. 1:12).

Finally, on her last day—due to shear weakness, one heard only the last words of her favorite Bible passage, "He is able to keep that which I have committed unto Him . . . " And just before her final breath she whispered only one word of her text: "Him, Him, Him!" How beautiful! She had everything she needed in Him, Him, Him! *And so do we!*

"I Know Whom I Have Believed"

(Based on 2 Tim. 1:12)

I may not see God's purpose for life's
Sorrows and its woe,
I may not know the reason
He retards my progress so,
But I know He has a purpose,
And I know my life is planned,
And I know my name is written
In the hollow of His hand.

I may not see the future
For it may be dark as night.
There may not be a glimmer
Of a star to give me light;
But I know that God still guides me,
And I know His way is sure,
And I know He'll walk beside me,
And His mercy shall endure.

I may not feel His pardon for the sins
I have confessed,
For feelings are deceitful,
But upon His Word I'll rest.
For I know His blood has cleansed me,
And I know He will receive,
(For His precious Word has told me)
Those who in His Word believe.

Esther A. Schumann

110

Noise! Noise! Noise!

Smog has often been emphasized as one of the chief pollutants and health hazards. Scientists are now telling us that noise is also a pollutant and is definitely affecting the health of many people.

We are told that noise can be distressful and disturbing to our equilibrium; and, also if the noise is great enough, vibrations can produce injury to the ear causing permanent damage. The irritability and annoyance from noise can also bring on increase in blood pressure and essential hypertension.

Just as continued noise can disturb the organs of the body, how often the rumblings of trouble disturb the calmness of the soul and bring disaster!

Scientists and engineers believe that there is every possibility that machinery can be designed which will diminish much of the noise from airplanes, trucks, compressors and even from household appliances. That is good news and we're grateful for it.

Speaking of household appliances, when I was a boy we didn't have an electric dishwasher, refrigerator, deep-freeze, washer, dryer, or furnace, air-conditioner, electric fans, mixers, humidifiers and dehumidifiers, exhaust fans, vacuum sweepers, radio, TV, etc. Think of all the noise produced by all of the above. However, I believe there must be good noise and bad noise! The other day our electricity was off for 6 hours. When it finally came back on-all the noise from the various electrical appliances was "music to our ears!"

We often think that power and strength lie in great noise; the noisier the object, the stronger it is. We immediately think of the deafening roar of a jet plane and the ear-splitting explosion of dynamite and the sharp clap of thunder.

The Scriptures, however, tell us that strength lies in silence. And Scripture knows. Isaiah 30:15 reminds us: "In quietness and in confidence shall be your strength." It is not the raging of the heathen that moves the world, nor the crashing of the mountains into the sea; it is rather the still small voice of God, which says, "Be still and know that I am God" (Ps. 46:10).

Christ had to get away from the continued noises of His day and retreat to the quiet mountainside. He asked His disciples to do likewise. He was not alone for long when, invariably, a noisy multitude caught up with Him. The moments that He had to Himself, however, He spent in prayer and quiet meditation with His heavenly Father. Also, in our daily devotion time and in the silence of worship lies our strength. Our problem is to remain quiet that God might speak.

At the end of His life, after the noisy screams and shouts of the mob, there was the silence of His crucifixion. The silence was broken by the victorious cry, "It is finished!" In that silence there is the strength of forgiveness, of peace, and of life forever for each one of us. Oh, yes, God's Word reminds us: "In quietness and in confidence shall be your strength" (Isa. 30:15).

While we will, no doubt, always have to put up with certain aggravating noises, how grateful we are that a remedy has already been found which can quiet the distressing noises and anxieties of the soul! The remedy is the Lord Jesus Christ Who assures us: "Peace I leave with you; My peace I give to you; not as the world gives do I give to you. Let not your hearts be troubled, neither let them be afraid." (John 14:27)

Thank God, there is peace and quiet for our souls. As the Lord Jesus calmed those angry waves on the Sea of Galilee with His mighty: "Peace, be still!" so He can calm the tempests that rage in our precious blood-bought souls. He loves us, He died for us and rose again; and now longs to be trusted by us through every trying circumstance as well as for our eternal salvation! His soothing Word to us is, "Be still and know that I am God." (Ps 46:10)

How vitally important it is that we faithfully and diligently listen to our God of peace as He comes to us through the "still, small voice" of the Holy Scriptures! Are we listening? Then blessed are we, for the Bible assures us: "Blessed are they that hear the Word of God and keep it" (Lk. 11:28).

Let us not allow the raucous noises of earth rob our souls of the joy and peace of hearing the "still, small voice" of our blessed Savior, JESUS.

Be still, my soul; the Lord is on your side;
Bear patiently the cross of grief or pain;
Leave to your God to order and provide;
In ev'ry change He faithful will remain.
Be still, my soul; your best, your heav'nly Friend
Thro' thorny ways leads to a joyful end.

Be still, my soul, tho' dearest friends depart
And all is darkened in the vale of tears;
Then shall you better know His love, His heart,
Who comes to soothe your sorrows and your fears.
Be still, my soul; your Jesus can repay
From His own fullness all He takes away.

Be still, my soul; the hour is hast'ning on
When we shall be forever with the Lord,
When disappointment, grief, and fear are gone,
Sorrow forgot, love's purest joys restored.
Be still, my soul; when change and tears are past,
All safe and blessed we shall meet at last. Amen

TLH 651

Bane and blessing, pain and pleasure,
By the Cross are sanctified
PEACE IS THERE THAT KNOWS NO MEASURE,
Joys that thro' all time abide.

TLH 354:4

A New Heart

In today's morning paper our eyes are directed to the news of organ transplants. How eagerly we watch to learn of success in this line. It is marvelous what science has done, and can do, and we rejoice over each victory. But as interesting and important as is the substitution of one organ for another, we are told in the Bible of another transplant, namely, "a new heart," which is even of greater consequence!

Checking a Bible Concordance, I note that the word "heart" is used approximately 900 times in the Bible. Sometimes it refers to the physical organ that pumps blood through the human system; but it is also widely used figuratively for the feelings, the will, and even the intellect; likewise for the center of anything.

The Bible speaks of the trembling, glad and searching heart; as well as the merry, wise and sorrowful heart. We also read of the wise, wicked and broken heart; the proud, sound, pure and heavy heart. In the Bible we are encouraged "to love the Lord with all our heart", and to follow, trust and seek Him with our whole heart. The word heart is used in the Scriptures as the seat of life or strength; hence it means mind, soul, spirit, or one's entire emotional nature and understanding.

Often when we speak of the heart we are referring to the attitude of the person. When we say, "have a heart!" we mean, "Be compassionate." When we say, "Her heart is right," we mean that her motives are pure.

The Bible reveals that the heart of natural mankind is not

inclined to turn to God for instruction or direction. Proverbs 19:3 says: "The foolishness of man subverts his way and ruins his affairs; then his heart is resentful and frets against the Lord."

The prophet Jeremiah said: "The heart is deceitful above all things, and desperately wicked; who can know it?" (Jer. 17:9) The Lord certainly knows it, and He said: "Out of the heart proceed evil thoughts, murders, adulteries, fornications, thefts, false witness, blasphemies; these are the things which defile a man." (Matt. 15:119-20)

As we look around us in the world we cannot deny that the natural heart of mankind is prone to evil. The wars, distress of nations about us, riots, rebellion against authority, rape, robbery, murder, and all the criminal tendencies which we see on every hand certainly confirm these Scriptures. It is evident that the natural man needs a change of heart, A NEW HEART, and none is exempt, for Romans 3:23 informs us that "All have sinned and come short of the glory of God."

Thus, at the center of every person's moral being there is a deceitful and defiling heart which cannot be replaced by another person's heart by transplantation, but it can be sanctified and purified by the Holy Spirit.

Here is truly good news! It is possible for the Lord God to give us A NEW HEART, absolutely free, gratis! Here is the glorious promise: "A NEW HEART will I give you, and a new spirit will I put within you" (Ez. 36:26).

Since the precious blood of the new covenant has been shed for the forgiveness of sins, God can righteously purify the heart of a believer by faith. (Acts 15:9) Truly, it will be A NEW HEART."

At the Apostolic Council held in Jerusalem, Peter rose up and declared: "Men and brethren, you know that a good while ago God made choice among us, that the Gentiles by my mouth should hear the word of the gospel, and believe. God, who knows the heart, acknowledged them, by giving them the Holy Spirit just as He did to us, and made no distinction between us and them, purifying their hearts by faith." (Acts 15:7-9)

The "gospel" which Peter mentioned is the good news of the death of Christ for our sins, His burial, and His resurrection for our justification. When that saving message is believed, by the power of the Holy Spirit, the believer's heart is purified by faith: it is A NEW HEART!

While the believer retains his old Adamic nature, he has been made a partaker of the divine nature (2 Peter 1:4), and is admonished to live according to the new nature, not the old, as we note in Colossians 3:12-17: "Therefore, as the elect of God, holy and beloved, put on tender mercies, kindness, humbleness of mind, meekness, longsuffering, bearing with one another, and forgiving one another, even as Christ forgave you, so you also must do, but above all these things put on love, which is the bond of perfection. And let the peace of God rule in your hearts, to which also you were called in one body; and be thankful. Let the Word of Christ dwell in you richly in all wisdom, teaching and admonishing one another in Psalms and hymns and spiritual songs, singing with grace in your hearts to the Lord. And whatever you do in word or deed, do all in the name of the Lord Jesus, giving thanks to God the Father through Him."

The Apostle John in writing to believers said: "If we confess our sins, He is faithful and just to forgive our sins, and to cleanse us from all unrighteousness." (1 John 1:9) And again: "The blood of Jesus Christ His Son cleanses us from all sin." (1 John 1:7) What could possibly be more fitting than to prayerfully sing:

Create in me a new heart, Lord,
That gladly I obey Your Word.
Let what You will be my desire,
And with new life my soul inspire.

Grant that I only You may love
And seek those things which are above
Till I behold You face to face,
O Light eternal, through Your grace. Amen

TLH 398:3,4

"God has two dwelling places: One in heaven and the other in a new, loving, trusting, thankful heart."

In What Direction Are We as a Nation Going?

Some years ago I came across the following: The average age of the world's great civilizations has been 200 years. These nations progressed through the following sequence.

1. From Bondage to Spiritual Faith
2. From Spiritual Faith to Great Courage
3. From Great Courage to Liberty
4. From Liberty to Abundance
5. From Abundance to Selfishness
6. From Selfishness to Complacency
7. From Complacency to Apathy
8. From Apathy to Dependence
9. From Dependence Back Again to Bondage

I would ask you, dear reader, does the trend look familiar?

In this regard, recall some passages of Scripture wherein the conditions characterizing the last days of the history of the Church on earth are revealed. For example, 2 Tim. 3:1-13: "This know also, that in the last days perilous times shall come. For men shall be lovers of their own selves, covetous, boasters, proud, blasphemers, disobedient to parents, unthankful, unholy, without natural affection, truce-breakers, false accusers, incontinent, fierce, despisers of those that are good, traitors, heady, high-minded, lovers of pleasures more than lovers of God;

having a form of godliness, but denying the power thereof; from such turn away . . . But evil men and seducers shall wax worse and worse, deceiving, and being deceived."

Edward Gibbon, in his monumental work, "The Decline and Fall of the Roman Empire," gave five basic reasons why that great civilization withered and died. These were:

1. The undermining of the dignity and sanctity of the home, which is the basis for human society.
2. "Higher and higher taxes; the spending of public money for free bread and circuses for the populace.
3. "The mad craze for pleasure; sports coming every year more exciting, more brutal, more immoral.
4. "The building of great armaments when the real enemy was within-the decay of individual responsibility.
5. "The decay of religion; faith fading into mere form, losing touch with life, losing power to guide the people."

In the light of these facts, does anyone have difficulty concluding that history is repeating itself?

"A man was complaining about his son. 'All day long he just runs around making noise, trying to get attention, and he just can't wait for recess. You'd think he would be better adjusted by now. After all, it is his third term in Congress.'"

America—A Sick Society?

In a Gallop Poll which was taken back in 1968, it was reported that forty-two percent of all Americans held the view that the United States was a "sick society"!

Some of the reasons given for these conclusions were: rioting, killing, lack of sufficient law enforcement, laxity of courts, breakdown in morals, shunning of religion and general selfishness.

When the prophet Isaiah wrote about conditions in the land of Israel, he used similar words regarding that nation. He said, "Ah, sinful nation, a people laden with iniquity, offspring of evildoers, sons who deal corruptly! They have forsaken the Lord, they have despised the Holy One of Israel, they are utterly estranged . . . Why will you still be smitten, that you continue to rebel? The whole head is sick, and the whole heart faint. From the sole of the foot even to the head, there is no soundness in it, but bruises and sores and bleeding wounds; they are not pressed out, or bound up, or softened with oil." (Isa. 1:4-6)

And what brought about this terrible condition in the land of Israel? The procuring cause of this national illness is stated by the prophet of God in these words: "They have forsaken the Lord." (v. 4)

Society is composed of individuals, and a nation is only as strong as or as weak as the individuals who make it up. And what is it that lifts up a nation, and that exalts it? Very clearly the Holy Scriptures declare: "Righteousness exalts a nation; but sin is a reproach to any people." (Prov. 14:34)

To those people who had turned away from God, He very graciously now extended the following cordial invitation through the prophet: "Come now, let us reason together, says the Lord: though your sins are like scarlet, they shall be as white as snow; though they are red like crimson, they shall become like wool. If you're willing and obedient, you shall eat the good of the land; But if you refuse and rebel, you shall be devoured by the sword; for the mouth of the Lord has spoken." (Isaiah 1:18-20)

Centuries after that invitation was given, the Lord Himself came to Palestine. The nation was under the iron heel of Rome and was still spiritually sick. Despite Israel's willful ignorance of the Lord's person and work, He graciously invited: "Come unto Me, all you that labor and are heavy laden, and I will give you rest." (Matt. 11:28)

There can be no successful denial of the genuineness of this loving invitation, for the Lord Jesus died for our sins and rose again for our justification, and now ever lives to make intercession for us. Whether the spiritual sickness is personal or national, the Lord Jesus Christ is the One and only sure and certain cure.

What are we as a nation, as families, and what are you as an individual, going to do about it?

Great King of nations, hear our prayer
While at Your feet we fall
And humbly with united cry
To You for mercy call.
The guilt is ours, but grace is Yours;
Oh, turn us not away,
But hear us from Your lofty throne
And help us Lord, we pray. Amen

Pro-Life

PRO is a Latin prefix meaning "on the side of, in favor of, in behalf of, "as in PRO-America. PRO-LIFE, therefore, means "on the side of life, in favor of life, in behalf of life." I'm FOR LIFE.

The opposite of PRO is CON or contra. CONTRA means "against, opposing, not in favor of, the CONtrary." In the current debate or CONTROversy, those favoring abortion do not call their position CONTRA-LIFE, which in fact it is; it's halting, bringing to an end, stopping life. Instead of calling it what it is, CONTRA-LIFE, they call it PRO-CHOICE, that is, on the side of choice. Their position is a call for CHOICE in a matter in which the holy Lord God does not give us a choice.

Pro-LIFE. Life is a word with many meanings. Basically, it means living, being alive, the quality that people, animals and plants have and that rocks and metals, etc. do not have.

LIFE is a gift of God. In the Creed we speak of the Holy Spirit as "the Lord and Giver of LIFE." The reference is both to the physical and spiritual LIFE. Two basic characteristics of LIFE, both physical and spiritual, are the ability to RELATE and to RESPOND. We relate to each other and to God, and we respond to the world around us and to the GOD WHO MADE US.

The opposite of life is DEATH. Death means separation. The dead are unable either to respond or relate to others or to God. A person may be physically alive but spiritually dead. Such people can respond and relate to those around them, but not to God. God created us FOR LIFE, to respond to His word, and to live in a relationship with Him and with others.

GOD FORBIDS THE TAKING OF LIFE. The Fifth Commandment says, "Thou shalt not kill." Positively it says "live and help live." The Fifth Commandment forbids all physical violence, murder, and suicide. It also forbids abortion as a means to end an unwanted pregnancy and euthanasia as a means of ending life no longer considered meaningful or viable. This commandment applies not only to those who are born, but also to those conceived but as yet unborn. In the Holy Scriptures God tells us in the most clear language that He set apart Jeremiah and appointed him as a prophet to the nations BEFORE he was born. We are told that John the Baptist "leaped for joy" in his mother's womb when Elizabeth and Mary greeted each other. (Luke 1:41, 44, and Luke 2:21)

In the Old Testament God said to His promised people: "I have set before you life and death, blessings and curses. Now CHOOSE LIFE, so that you and your children may LIVE." In the New Testament Jesus says: "I am come that they might have LIFE and have it more abundantly." Even if we had the choice, which PRO-CHOICE people advocate, God has already told us what our choice should be: "CHOOSE LIFE!" The Lord God, our Maker and Redeemer is PRO-LIFE.

Our Church Body has taken a strong PRO-LIFE position. As God's people we need to inform ourselves concerning this struggle in all of its aspects. We need to support PRO-LIFE GROUPS. We need to examine the positions of those we elect to public office; and we need to pray and work to the end that this matter GOD'S WILL MAY BE DONE AMONG US. God, through His blessed

Son, Jesus, our Savior and Lord, has blessed us with ETERNAL LIFE. In response, let's make use of every opportunity to be PRO-LIFE to CHOOSE LIFE through His most Holy Name.

Pray and ponder the following:

"You, O Lord, are my hope, my trust, O Lord, from my youth. Upon You I have leaned from my birth; You are He Who took me from my mother's womb. My praise is continually of You." (Ps. 71:5,6)

"You formed my inward parts; You knit me together in my mother's womb . . . My frame was not hidden from You when I was being made in secret . . . Your eyes behold my unformed substance; in Your book were written, every one of them, the days that were formed for me, when as yet there was none of them." (Ps. 139:13f)

"As you do not know how the Spirit comes to the bones in the womb of a woman with child, so you do not know the work of God Who makes everything." (Eccl. 11:5)

"Thus says the Lord Who made you, Who formed you from the womb and will help you." (Isa. 44:2)

"Thus says the Lord, your Redeemer, Who formed you from the womb; I am the Lord, Who made all things . . ." (Isa. 44:24)

"Before I formed you in the womb I knew you, and before you were born I consecrated you; I appointed you a prophet to the nations." (Jer. 1:5)

"Listen to Me, O house of Jacob, all the remnant of the house of Israel, who have been borne by Me from your birth, carried from the womb; even to your old age I am He, and to gray hairs I will carry you. I have made, and I will bear; I will carry and will save." (Isa. 46:3,4)

"Listen to Me, O coastlands, and listen, you peoples from afar. The Lord called me from the womb, from the body of my mother He named my name." (Isa. 49:1)

"And now the Lord says, Who formed me from the womb to be His servant, to bring Jacob back to Him, and that Israel might be gathered to Him, for I a honored in the eyes of the Lord, and my God has become my strength . . ." (Isa. 49:5)

"I believe in God the Father Almighty, Maker of heaven and earth. What does this mean? I believe that God HAS MADE ME AND ALL CREATURES; that He has given me my body and soul, eyes, ears, and all my members, my reason and all my senses, and still preserves them . . . For all which it is my duty to thank and praise, to serve and obey Him." (Luther's Explanation of the First Article of the Apostles' Creed)

Right to Life:
Diary of an Unborn Child

Oct. 5: Today my life began. My parents do not know it yet. I am as small as a seed of an apple, but it is me already. And I am to be a girl. I shall have blond hair and blue eyes. Just about everything is settled, though, even the fact that I shall love flowers.

Oct. 19: Some say that I am not a real person yet, that only my mother exists. But I am a real person, just as a small crumb of bread is yet truly bread. My mother is. I am.

Oct. 23: My mouth is just beginning to open now. Just think, in a year or so I shall be laughing and later talking. I know what my first word will be: Mama.

Oct. 25: My heart began to beat today all by itself. From now on it will gently beat for the rest of my life without ever stopping to rest! And after many years it will tire. It will stop, and then I shall die.

Nov. 2: I am growing a bit every day. My arms and legs are beginning to take shape. But I have to wait a long time yet before those little legs will race me to my mother's arms; before these little arms will be able to gather flowers and embrace my father.

Nov. 12: Tiny fingers are beginning to form on my hands. Funny how small they are! I'll be able to fold them in prayer some day to thank God for my mommy and daddy.

Nov. 20: It wasn't until today that the doctor told Mom that I am living here under her heart. Oh, how happy she must be! Are you happy, Mommy?

Nov. 25: My mom and dad are probably thinking of a name for me. But they don't even know that I am a little girl. I want to be called Kathy. I am getting so big already.

Dec. 10: My hair is growing. It is smooth and bright and shiny. I wonder what kind of hair Mom has.

Dec. 13: I am just about able to see. It is dark around me. When Mom brings me into the world it will be full of sunshine and flowers. But what I want more than anything is to see my mom. How do you look, Mom?

Dec. 24: I wonder if Mom hears the whispering of my heart? Some children come into the world a little sick. But my heart is strong and healthy. It beats so strongly: tup-tup, tup-tup. You"ll have a healthy little daughter, Mom!

Dec. 28: Today my mother killed me.

Author Unknown

There is a law in our country that states it is perfectly legal to be CONTRA-LIFE, and to kill a child. Kill an eagle and there is an immediate fine up to $250,000 and two years in prison. Lord, have mercy!

Beauty for Ashes

Years ago West Berlin conceived and perfected a plan to convert a mountain of rubble and refuse into a delightful recreation area. This "mountain" is now being used as a ski area with numerous ski jumps and also a toboggan run. What a change!

When living in Indianapolis, I ministered to a shut-in who, by an intercom system, managed a refuse dump. Today expensive houses with beautiful yards cover the area. What a transformation!

The same is true of an area here in Bloomington where a landfill of 25 years ago is today a quiet neighborhood of beautiful houses, lawns, flowers and trees. What a difference!

One of our large cities that discards thousands of tons of refuse daily has a plan to compact, sanitize and deodorize the refuse, cover it with layers of soil, and develop it with nature and hiking trails and other recreation uses. What a contrast!

Beauty instead of refuse! What an antithesis! I am reminded of the Bible expression: "Beauty for ashes." The Book of Isaiah was written some seven hundred years before our blessed Savior, Jesus Christ, was born, yet we know from Luke 4:18 that Isaiah 61:1-3 was written prophetically of Him! He said, "The Spirit of the Lord God is upon me; because the Lord has anointed me to preach good tidings unto the meek; He has sent me to bind up the broken-hearted, to proclaim liberty to the captives, and the opening of the prison to them that are bound; to proclaim the acceptable year of the Lord, and the day of vengeance of our God; to comfort all that mourn; to appoint unto them that mourn in Zion, to give unto them BEAUTY FOR ASHES, the oil of joy for mourning, the garment of praise for the spirit of heaviness; that they might be called trees of righteousness, the planting of the Lord, that He might be glorified."

Does life ever seem wasted and useless? Even for those who may have bitterly misspent their years, Christ is the One who can bring about a glorious change— BEAUTY FOR ASHES! He can, so to speak, sanitize and deodorize—cleanse and sweeten life—yours and mine.

We all have failed times without number, yet He loves us and longs to bring "good tidings to the meek . . . bind up the brokenhearted, proclaim liberty to the captives . . . give freedom to the imprisoned . . . comfort all who mourn," and instead of ashes, He wants to give beauty! Oh, yes, Christ Jesus longs to give us BEAUTY FOR ASHES!

He is worthy of our trust for He died for our sins and rose again for our justification, and He longs for the response of faith and love from us. Here and now, invite Him into your heart:

Enter now my waiting heart,
Glorious King and Lord most holy.
Dwell in me and never leave,
Though I am but poor and lowly.
What vast riches will be mine
When you are my guest divine!

LW 34:2

May BEAUTY FOR ASHES be yours!

"It's not who I am, but whose I am that counts."

Only Sheep
Have a Shepherd

The Bible does not give a flattering picture of what we are like when it refers to us as sheep. No doubt we would prefer to think of ourselves as being more like some other animals.

Some of you have been given a great deal of intellectual ability, for example. Unconsciously you may desire your friends to say, "He's as wise as an owl and as sharp as a fox." But, you see, owls and foxes don't have shepherds—only sheep do.

Others of you have a pleasing personality and may think of yourselves as "social lions." And that's fine except that lions don't have a shepherd—in fact, sometimes lions need tamers. Only sheep have a shepherd.

Still others, probably the majority of us, do not claim to be wise as owls nor are we social lions. And yet we may accomplish even more than those having more natural gifts simply because we "work like a horse." However, horses don't have shepherds. The fact still remains that only sheep have a shepherd.

We could, no doubt, continue this menagerie to include the way each of us would best like to characterize himself/herself. All such comparing must cease, however, as we stand before God, before whom we are weak, helpless, wandering sheep. However, that is only one half of the picture. Blessed are they who can also confidently say, sing and pray, THE LORD IS MY SHEPHERD!

He Leadeth Me

In pastures green? Not always.
Sometimes He who knoweth best
In kindness leadeth me in weary ways,
Where heavy shadows be.
Out of the sunshine, warm and soft, and bright,
Out of the sunshine, into darkest night.
I oft would faint with sorrow and affright,
Only for this—I know He holds my hand.
So whether in green or desert land,
I trust, although I may not understand.

And by still waters? No, not always so;
Oft times the heavy tempests round me blow.
And o'er my soul the waves and billows go.
But when the storm beats loudest and
I cry aloud for help, the Master standeth by,
And whispers in my soul:
"Lo, it is I."
Above the tempest wild I hear Him say,
"Beyond the darkness lies the perfect day.
In every path of thine, I lead the way."

So whether on the hilltops high and fair I dwell,
Or in the sunless valleys where the shadows lie—
What matter? He is there.
And more than this.
Where'er the pathway leads
He gives to me no broken, helpless reed,
But His own hand, sufficient in my need.
So where He leads me, I can safely go,
And in the blest hereafter, I shall know
Why, in His kindness, He hath led me so.

-Author Unknown

Because the Lord Is My Shepherd—
I Shall Not Want

"I shall not want" - REST:
> *"He maketh me to lie down in green pastures."*

"I shall not want" - PEACE:
> *"He leadeth me beside the still waters."*

"I shall not want" - MERCY:
> *"He restoreth my soul."*

"I shall not want" - GUIDANCE:
> *"He leadeth me in the paths of righteousness for His name's sake."*

"I shall not want" - COURAGE:
> "Yea, though I walk through the valley of the shadow of death, I will fear no evil."

"I shall not want" - COMPANIONSHIP:
> *"For Thou art with me."*

"I shall not want" - COMFORT:
> *"Thy rod and Thy staff they comfort me."*

"I shall not want" - VICTORY:
> *"Thou preparest a table before me in the presence of my enemies."*

"I shall not want" - GLADNESS:
> *"Thou anointest my head with oil."*

"I shall not want" - SATISFACTION:
> *"My cup runneth over."*

"I shall not want" - ANYTHING IN LIFE:
> *"Surely goodness and mercy shall follow me all the days of my life."*

"I shall not want" - ANYTHING IN THE LIFE TO COME:
> "And I will dwell in the house of the Lord forever."

- Bible Society Record

Psalm Twenty-Three

The 23rd Psalm has been a source of comfort to myriads of people in life and in death. Consider the following outline, and allow the Psalm to become a source of life and comfort to you, regardless of your circumstances and surroundings.

The Lord is my Shepherd - Perfect Salvation.
I shall not want - Perfect Satisfaction.
He maketh me to lie in green pastures - Perfect Rest.
He leadeth me beside still waters - Perfect Refreshment.
He restoreth my soul - Perfect Restoration.
He leadeth me in paths of righteousness -
    Perfect Protection.
Thou art with me - Perfect Company.
Thy rod and Thy staff - Perfect Comfort.
Thou preparest a table - Perfect Provision.
Thou anointest my head - Perfect Consecration.
My cup runneth over - Perfect Joy.
Goodness and mercy shall follow me - Perfect Care.
I will dwell . . . forever - Perfect Destiny.

Thought you'd like the following:

Pastor to congregation: "We will now join in speaking together the twenty-third Psalm, and will the person who usually gets to the 'still waters' while the rest of us are yet in 'green pastures' please wait and go with the crowd?"

Crossing the Stream

For a time little Emily was very ill. Baffled at the deadly course of the disease, the doctor finally said to the mother and father, "Nothing but prayer can save your child." As he closed the door and walked out into the night, mother and father fell on their knees and begged God to spare their only child. All night they prayed as they had never prayed before. But God had other plans. He took little Emily to Himself in heaven.

For some years before the loss of their little one, the parents had stopped coming to church. They realized the importance of religion for little Emily, had her baptized, regularly sent her to Sunday School; but they themselves attended church only at Christmastime to hear Emily recite her piece, and at Easter. Now, when they needed the church most they stayed away altogether. On Sundays they went to the beach or mountains or woods— anywhere except church.

One Sunday, while they were on such an outing, they watched a shepherd trying to make his flock of sheep cross a stream. He got behind them and tried to drive them across, but they would not go. Then he got in front of them and tried to lead them across. Still they would not follow. Finally the shepherd picked up a baby lamb from its mother's side and with it in his arms, he waded into the stream. Immediately the mother sheep plunged in after the shepherd, and the rest of the flock followed. All safely crossed the foaming waters.

"Why, that's what God is trying to do to us," the man said to his wife. "He wants us to go to heaven and be with Him. By taking our Emily to heaven, He knows that heaven will be so much dearer to us. He wants us to meet her there. We might as well be honest with ourselves. We forsook the Lord, and this is His way of bringing us back to Him."

- P. C. Neipp

'Twas a Sheep

'Twas a sheep, not a lamb, that went astray
In the parable Jesus told.
'Twas a grown-up sheep that wandered away
From the ninety and nine in the fold.

And out in the hilltops and out in the cold,
'Twas a sheep that the Good Shepherd sought,
And back to the flock and back to the fold
'Twas a sheep that the Good Shepherd brought.

Now, why should the sheep be so carefully fed
And cared for still today?
Because there is danger, if they go wrong,
They will lead the lambs astray;

For the lambs will follow the sheep, you know,
Wherever they wander, wherever they go.
If the sheep go wrong, it will not be long
Till the lambs are as wrong as they.

So still with the sheep we must earnestly plead
For the sake of the lambs today.
If the lambs are lost, what a terrible cost
Some sheep will have to pay.

- Author Unknown

When Doubts Arise

Where do we turn when doubts arise in our minds about our salvation?

There are many passages in Scripture that embrace teachings of comfort. There is the doctrine of God's universal grace, of our redemption through Christ, of our justification by grace for Christ's sake through faith, and so forth.

However, there is another article of faith we should not overlook. In Ephesians 1:4 the Apostle Paul states: *"He (the Father) chose us in Him (Christ) before the foundation of the world."* This refers to the glorious doctrine of the "election of grace," also called "predestination."

In eternity, long before the creation of the world, you and I already existed in the mind of God. He knew us by name. In His grace He chose us to be His own, knowing that He would redeem us from sin and death through His Son, and through the Holy Spirit He would bring us to faith and keep us in faith.

This is why Jesus could say: *"My sheep hear My voice, and I know them, and they follow Me; and I give unto them eternal life, and they shall never perish, neither shall any man pluck them out of My hand" (John 10: 27-28).*

Paul states: *"Whom He did predestinate, them He also called; and whom He called, them He also justified; and whom He justified, them He also glorified" (Rom. 8:30).* In other words, God has decreed our salvation and nothing, *"neither death, nor life, nor angels, nor principalities, nor things present, nor things to come, nor powers, nor height, nor depth, nor anything else in all creation, will be able to separate us from the love of God in Christ Jesus our Lord" (Rom. 8:39f.).*

This teaching is pure Gospel and intended to comfort those who are troubled by their sin. Never regard this as part of God's Law.

Nor should this teaching be used to make us carnally secure so that we say: "I have it made! I am one of the elect! I can do as I please and sin to my heart's content." If we were to think that, then we would need the Law to crush and humble us again. We are warned and admonished, *"Let anyone who thinks that he stands take heed lest he fall" (1 Cor. 10:12).*

On the other hand, when properly used, there is not a more comforting doctrine in Scripture than that we are God's elect children in Christ. When we are troubled, distressed or in doubt about our salvation, waste no time in fleeing to the gracious, inviting arms of our Heavenly Father who says: *"Fear not, for I have redeemed you, I have called you by your name, you are Mine" (Isa. 43:1).*

From eternity, O God,
In Thy Son Thou didst elect me;
Therefore, Father, on life's road
Graciously to heav'n direct me;
Send to me Thy Holy Spirit
That His gifts I may inherit.

TLH 411:1

Speak, and Hold
Not Your Peace

Why is it that we are so reluctant to talk to others about Jesus and our faith in Him, to share the joy of our salvation, and to invite them to our church to meet our Savior? For some reason it appears that the idea has gained credence that religion is a private matter; something you are not supposed to talk about.

Perhaps part of the reason for this is the fact that too many have accepted the great American heresy which says that all religions have some good in them, and that it does not make so much difference what one believes so long as you are sincere in your belief. Following that type of reasoning, one church is as good as the other.

That, of course, goes counter to what the Holy Scriptures teach. Christianity is a very exclusive religion in which Jesus says: *"I am the Way, the Truth and the Life; no one comes to the Father but by Me"* *(John 14:6).*

The Apostle Peter told the Jewish Council: *"Neither is there salvation in any other, for there is no other name under heaven given among men whereby we can be saved except in the name of Jesus"* *(Acts 4:12).*

The Apostle Paul by inspiration writes: *"There is one God and one Mediator between God and man, the Man Christ Jesus"* *(1 Tim. 2:5).*

If we really believe *Romans 10:9 "that if you confess with your mouth the Lord Jesus, and believe in your heart that God has raised Him from the dead, you will be saved,"* then SURELY WE HAVE NO CHOICE BUT TO SHARE THAT MESSAGE.

We might be surprised how many people would be open to our witness. We might be amazed by how many people, through the power of the Spirit, could be persuaded to accept our invitation to "come and see" (John 1:46).

The story is told that Henry Ford had once purchased a large insurance policy—a fact that soon became known to the public. One of Ford's long-time friends, who was in the insurance business, heard about it. Completely surprised by the purchase, since he had not heard that Ford was in the market for insurance, the friend went to see Ford and asked if the story was true. Ford told his friend that it was true, that he had, indeed, purchased the policy. The friend asked why he hadn't purchased the policy from him since he was a personal friend and had been for many years. Ford simply replied: "You never asked me."

Could it be that there are people we know who are not Christian; who are missing out on the joy and peace of Christ simply because we haven't shared with them? Could it be that we are saying "no" for some who may be waiting to say "yes" if we would only ask? What a needless tragedy that people are not prepared for death and eternity simply because we have never asked them or shared the message of salvation with them!

In this connection we might well read the account in 2 Kings, chapters 6 and 7, about the lepers during the famine when Israel was under siege. When they found the wealth of provisions in the deserted camp of the Syrians and had eaten their fill, they were conscience stricken and said*: "We're not doing right. This is a day of good news and we are keeping it to ourselves" (2 Kings 7:9a).*

The other day I heard this definition of evangelism. "Evangelism is one beggar telling another beggar where he found bread."

By the grace and mercy of a benevolent God we know Jesus, the Bread of life. We have no other choice but to SPEAK, AND HOLD NOT OUR PEACE, always beginning with those with whom we live and branching out to friends, co-workers, neighbors, etc.

Many of us are familiar with the Miranda Act which instructs all police officers to give the arrested parties a review of their rights as a United States citizen. The one line most of us can remember the best is "You have the right to remain silent; anything you say can and will be used against you in a court of law . . ." The first time you hear these words spoken in person, you realize the gravity of the situation.

In a very different way believers in the Lord Jesus Christ are asked a different sort of question by the Holy Spirit in our hearts. We are questioned about our faith and trust in the Lord God for our eternal salvation on a daily basis by the world, and commanded to witness for the Lord in His holy Word. As a recent songwriter wrote: "You don't have the right to remain silent if you have been arrested by God's grace."

The truth is that we are commanded in the Scriptures that we do not have the right to remain silent about our faith. Believers in the Lord Jesus Christ are called to tell the world about Christ's death, resurrection and His saving grace, and to tell again and again how we have been pardoned for our sins. In 1 Peter 3:15 we are urged: *"In your hearts set apart Christ as Lord. Always be prepared to give an answer to everyone who asks you to give the reason for the hope that you have."*

How can we be silent about the hope, peace and joy of knowing Christ as our Lord and Savior? Share Him! Share Him! SPEAK, AND HOLD NOT YOUR PEACE!

Shocking, but True

You lived next door to me for years,
We shared our dreams, our joys and tears,
A friend to me you were indeed,
A friend who helped me when in need.

My faith in you was strong and sure.
We had such trust as should endure.
No spats between us ever rose,
Our friends were alike—and so, our foes.

What sadness, then, my friend to find,
That after all, you weren't so kind.
The day my life on earth did end
I found you weren't a faithful friend.

For all those years we spent on earth
You never talked of second birth.
You never spoke of my lost soul,
And of the Christ who'd make me whole!

I plead today from hell's cruel fire,
And tell you now my least desire—
You cannot do a thing for me—
No words today my bonds will free.

But - do not err, my friend, again—
Do all you can for souls of men.
Plead with them now quite earnestly—
Lest they descend and be with me!

- Lutheran Witness, 10-3-61

Be Still, and Know That I Am God

Isn't it strange how a simple, common experience can suddenly take on new and profound significance? Take the matter of dropping pebbles into a pond. Practically every man who was once a boy has done it, and many a lady who was once a girl. Dropping pebbles into a pond—I did it the other afternoon with unexpected fascination.

Far back in the woods where summer flowers bloomed and grasses grew with little fear that anyone would step on them, I came upon a sleeping pond—"still waters, silent as a shadow." The mirror-like surface reflected almost perfectly the glory of the trees in their red, yellow and green Fall finery and the peace of the white clouds sailing lazily on a blue sky over Owen County, Indiana.

The long concert by the frogs and crickets, birds, and katydids was over for another season. The stillness was like a lullaby sung by Mother Nature as she put the plants, the bugs and the little animals to sleep.

It was a good place to drop anchor for a while and give the mind a brief repose to wander and to wonder where and how it would. I thought of God and His much needed admonition: "Be still, and know that I am God." I thought of Christ, standing in the storm, and the angry waves losing all their fury in obedience to His exacting command, "Peace, be still!"

A leaf fell in a long glide and landed on the pond. It sent a series of ever-widening circles over the water, rippling the surface and distorting the reflection.

I tossed a pebble into the pond. Large circles ruffled the surface and the reflection was almost lost. I heaved a stump into the pond. The waters protested with a resounding splash, shattering the silence and completely destroying the reflection. For a long time the waters were riled, confused, frustrated, resentful and muddy.

How like a pond is the mind of man! It can—oh, yes, it can reflect the glory of God in life. The mind of man was meant to be serene and clear and good, like a pond far back in the woods. But the leaves of irritation gliding in, pebbles of disappointments, stones of frustration, and boulders of calamity are continually dropping into it— disturbing and shattering its tranquility, distorting and destroying its reflection, leaving it frustrated, confused, irritated, exasperated and muddy.

There is so little silence, stillness and serenity in this world of ours. If all the sounds that beat upon our ears in a single day were concentrated into one great noise, the thunder of it, I'm sure, would be most deafening.

The woods behind our house are getting smaller and the roar of history louder and louder. Man has improved almost everything but the silence and the solitude he so desperately needs to soothe his mind, his body, his heart and his soul.

True, God can speak in the howl and thunder of the storm—and He sometimes does. But usually He fashions His wonders in silence. For example, the seasons move along as quietly as a cat walking on velvet. The sun sets like a baby falling asleep. The evening star appears without fanfare.

Was it merely coincidence that Christ grew and lived where He could catch sight of the Great Sea, where He could gaze unhindered at the starry heavens and where He could walk through peaceful valleys and sit by restful waters, where He could preach on hillsides and climb to mountaintops to be alone with His Father? I think not.

We are surrounded by man-made scenes of pain and conflict that exhaust our courage and our strength; that take so much of the joy out of our living. The very air we breathe is often heavy with fears, frustrations and anxieties.

Our great need—without question—is for a place of retreat, anywhere but somewhere. Our great need is for moments of silence, anytime, when passions and desires, sorrows and grief, stings of meanness and ingratitudes, dreams that never jell, frustrations of unfinished jobs, pressures of society and tensions of responsibility, torments of self-pity can all be laid down to rest a while like waves on stormy Galilee when Christ spoke out His, "Peace, be still!"

Our great need is for a sacred place and time of solitude away from the hurly-burly of life, where we can go, often and regularly, not to escape the battles of living, but to prepare ourselves for them. Where we can think on things that are good and true and firm and lovely, and which will always be that way. Where God's truth can be seen more clearly. Where we can be alone with our Lord in prayer. Where we can be alone with Him and His precious Word of comfort and truth.

There is such a place. No long journey or any strenuous effort on our part is required. A Call or an assignment to another field, a change of position, a move to another area isn't necessarily the answer. Really, the place is where you are. It may be a certain corner in your room. It may be in your study or in your car. It could be in your favorite chair by the window. It could be a little pond back in the woods—an area referred to as Sunshine Acres—or it very well could be right here where we are meeting at our District office in Fort Wayne. In short, it can be any time and any place where we can be alone with our Lord and Savior and His sacred, saving Word, and in His amazing grace have Him lay His hand upon our hearts and whisper, "Be still, and know that I am God!"

- A.C.O.

Be still, my soul; the Lord is on thy side;
Bear patiently the cross of grief or pain;
Leave to thy God to order and provide;
In ev'ry change He faithful will remain.
Be still, my soul; thy best, thy heav'nly, Friend
Thro' thorny ways leads to a joyful end.

TLH 651:1

Two Creations

I was reading of a meeting of the American Society of Newspaper Editors in Washington, D.C., where a prominent astronomer informed the gathering that the question of the origin of the universe is still unsettled. The astronomers cannot agree whether the universe started with a gigantic explosion billions of years ago, or whether matter is being continually created. The speaker said serious obstacles were in the path of both theories. Well, I guess so!

Since the astronomers have only unproven theories and admit they do not know how the universe originated, the question comes: Why not accept the facts stated by One who certainly knows whereof He speaks? What is more, He was there in the beginning! When we "just don't know," then we should go to the Source Book—the Answer Book—the Holy Bible. There we read that the Father said to the Son, *"In the beginning, O Lord, You laid the foundations of the earth, and the heavens are the work of Your hands" (Heb. 1:10).* Of the Son it is also said: *"For by Him all things were created: things in heaven and on earth, visible and invisible, whether thrones or powers or rulers or authorities; all things were created by Him and for Him. He is before all things, and IN HIM ALL THINGS HOLD TOGETHER" (Col. 1:16-17).*

Regarding the explosion theory, from what we know of explosions would you say that explosions hold things together? Would you say that explosions of any kind possess constructive or destructive powers? What do you know, or have, or see that came into being by an explosion? How ridiculous! To what nonsensical extremes some people will go to try to eliminate the holy, almighty Lord God as the Creator of heaven and earth!

Of the Son of God it is written: *"He was in the world, and the world WAS MADE BY HIM"* *(John 1:10).* Rightly do Christians faithfully confess: "I believe in God the Father Almighty, MAKER OF HEAVEN AND EARTH AND OF ALL THINGS VISIBLE AND INVISIBLE."

A little paper clipping that I retrieved from one of my files says it exactly. The title is: A Computer's Answer as to How the World Came into Being. "In a multi-billion dollar project to determine what actually happened when the earth was created, scientists and engineers spent years gathering information. As the thousands of bits of information came in, they were fed into a giant computer. Finally, the great day came: all the information had been programmed. The scientists and engineers gathered around the great computer as the instruction was punched in: Produce a detailed account of the creation of the earth. Breathlessly, the group waited. The great computer hummed, rattled and finally the printer typed out, *'See Genesis 1:1.'*"

And as you know, Genesis 1:1 reads for all people of all times, "In the beginning GOD CREATED THE HEAVENS AND THE EARTH." Oh, yes, *"By the Word of the Lord were the heavens made, their starry host by the breath of His mouth . . . For He spoke, and it came to be; He commanded, and it stood firm"* *(Ps. 33:6,9).* *"By Him all things were created: things in heaven and on earth, visible and invisible"* *(Col. 1:16).* Of the Son of God it is written: *"He was in the world, and the world was made through Him."*

Beautiful Savior, King of Creation,
Son of God and Son of Man!
Truly I'd love Thee, Truly I'd serve Thee,
Light of my soul, my Joy, my Crown.

TLH 657:1

Interesting, exciting, fascinating and miraculous as the creation of the world (physical universe) is, there is a creation even more interesting, impressive, thrilling and heart-stirring, as revealed in 2 Corinthians 5:17f.: *"If any one is in Christ, HE IS A NEW CREATION; the old has passed away; behold, the new has come. All this is from God, who through Christ reconciled us to Himself and gave us the ministry of reconciliation."* And the substance of that "ministry" is that Christ was delivered for our offences, and was raised again for our justification. Therefore, *"being justified by faith, we have peace with God through our Lord Jesus Christ"* (Rom. 4:25 and 5:1).

And because of this "new creation" brought about in us, we and all believers can say: *"We are His workmanship, created in Christ Jesus for good works, which God prepared in advance for us to do" (Eph. 2:10).*

All who believe and are baptized
Shall see the Lord's salvation;
Baptized into the death of Christ,
We are His new creation.
Through Christ's redemption we shall stand
Among the glorious heav'nly band
Of ev'ry tribe and nation.

- Adapted

All believers in the Lord Jesus Christ make up the holy Christian Church, the communion of saints. And of the Church we sing:

The Church's one foundation
Is Jesus Christ, her Lord;
She is his NEW CREATION
By water and the Word.

From heav'n he came and sought her
To be his holy bride;
With his own blood he bought her,
And for her life he died.

LW 289:1

What can we say: What can we do? How can we respond to THE GOD OF ALL CREATION?

All praise to God, who reigns above,
THE GOD OF ALL CREATION,
The God of wonders, pow'r, and love,
The God of our salvation!
With healing balm my soul He fills,
The God who ev'ry sorrow stills,
TO GOD ALL PRAISE AND GLORY!

TLH 19:1

Cynic: "I could have made a better world than this."
Sage: "That is why God put you here. Go to it!"

The Heavens Declare God's Glory

The spacious firmament on high,
With all the blue celestial sky,
And spangled heavens a shining frame,
Their great origin now proclaim.

Th' unwearied sun, from day to day,
Does its Creator's power display,
And publishes to every land
The work of an Almighty hand.

Soon as the evening shades prevail,
The moon takes up the wondrous tale,
And nightly to the listening earth
Repeats the story of its birth.

While all the stars that round it burn,
And all the planets in their turn,
Confirm the tidings as they roll,
And spread the truth from pole to pole.

What though, in solemn silence, all
Move round this dark terrestrial ball?
What though no real voice nor sound
Amid their radiant spheres be found?

In reason's ear they all rejoice,
And utter forth a glorious voice;
Forever singing, as they shine,
"The hand that made us is Divine."

The Monkey's Viewpoint

Three monkeys sat in a coconut tree
Discussing things as they're said to be.
Said one to the others, "Now listen, you two,
There's a certain rumor that can't be true,
That man descended from our noble race—
The very idea is a disgrace.

"No monkey ever deserted his wife,
Starved her babies and ruined her life.
And you've never known another monk
To leave her babies with others to bunk,
Or pass them on from one to another
Till they scarcely knew who is their mother.

"And another thing, you'll never see
A monk build a fence around a coconut tree
And let the coconuts go to waste,
Forbidding all other monks a taste.
Why if I'd put a fence around the tree,
Starvation would force you to steal from me!

"Here's another thing a monk won't do—
Get out at night and get on a stew,
Or use a gun or club or knife
To take some other monkey's life.
Yes, man descended, the ornery cuss,
But, brother, he didn't descend from us."

Anon

158

Him We Can Trust

Dwight L. Moody, a renowned evangelist of yesteryear, had spoken long and earnestly to a young man who had come to him seeking relief from a burden of guilt. In an effort to assure the young man of God's readiness to forgive those who repent and believe, the kindly evangelist had quoted a number of the blessed Savior's precious promises. Among the many passages he had quoted were the Savior's words of invitation and promise: *"Come unto Me, all you that labor and are heavy laden, and I will give you rest"* (Matt. 11:28).

Disconsolate and unable to find comfort in any of the quoted passages, the young man exclaimed in desperation: "I just can't believe!" To which the evangelist was quick to reply: "Whom can't you believe?" The young man sat silent for a moment. The words of the wise evangelist had struck home. Suddenly it dawned upon the penitent young sinner that it was CHRIST whom he was refusing to believe; Christ, and not the kindly gentleman before him! And with that realization came the first stirring of a new-found faith.

It was Christ, and not Dwight L. Moody, who *had said: "Take My yoke upon you, and learn of Me; for I am meek and lowly in heart; and you shall find rest unto your souls. For My yoke is easy and My burden is light"* (Matt. 11:29f.).

How important that we learn and re-learn the lesson that young man took home with him that night! In the church as we know it today it is so easy, unconsciously perhaps, for us to base our hope for heaven on what the pastor says, or what the Sunday school and Bible class teachers say, or on what the catechism says, or on the latest pronouncement of a church body.

All of these, of course, are important and have their rightful place, but in the hour of trial, in the day of temptation, on a sickbed, or when the angel of death is hovering around, we will want to know, above all else, what our blessed Savior, the Lord Jesus Christ, says. IT IS HE AND HE ALONE WHO IS WORTHY OF OUR ULTIMATE TRUST! For He and He alone is the omnipotent, omniscient, omnipresent "Word of God Incarnate."

It is Christ, the one and only Savior, who tells us: *"He that hears My Word and believes on Him that sent Me HAS EVERLASTING LIFE"* *(John 5:24).* It is the eternal Christ, and no mere man, who has given us the sublime assurance: *"I am the Resurrection and the Life; he that believes in Me though he were dead, yet shall he live; and whosoever lives and believes in Me shall never die"* *(John 11:25).*

Through the power of the Holy Spirit, Him we can trust, Him we can believe. On Him we stake our souls for time and for all eternity.

Trust Him when dark doubts assail you;
Trust Him when your strength is small;
Trust Him when simply to trust Him
Seems the hardest thing of all.
Trust Him, He is ever faithful;
Trust Him, for His will is best;
Trust Him, for the heart of Jesus
Is the only place of rest.
"In You, O Lord, do I put my trust." (Ps. 71:10)

Standing on the Oxygen Line

The story is told of a doctor who was about to perform an operation. The patient had been made ready; the oxygen mask was in place; the valves were opened and everything seemed ready to proceed, except that the patient wasn't getting oxygen. Nothing could proceed without a flow of oxygen. Oxygen is vital. No one can live without it. One of the nurses, detecting the problem said, rather timidly, "Doctor, you are standing on the oxygen line!" While the doctor was present with the best of intentions; while he was determined to help the patient in the best way he knew; he was not aware of the fact that he was the obstacle to survival. He was standing on the oxygen line.

Could it be that we, at times, might actually be hindrances to someone's spiritual survival or even to our own? This is such a perfect parallel for us to check our lives to see if we, unknowingly, might be an obstacle to someone's—perhaps our own—spiritual life and growth, even survival, because we are standing on the spiritual oxygen line.

What are some ways in which we might be such an obstacle? I will mention several, and I am certain you will be able to name others. Here are just a few:

When the call to worship is made and we offer some lame excuse not to join fellow believers in Christ-centered worship, we are standing on the oxygen line to our own faith and spiritual well-being. We are actually hindering our own spiritual life and growth. We are depriving ourselves of the "life abundant" the Lord holds out to us.

Or let us say that we come to church, but fail to prepare ourselves to be in the presence of our blessed Savior. Again, we are standing on the oxygen line, and we will leave as empty as we came.

Or we are busier than the Lord ever intended for us to be and so we are left with little or no time for feeding our precious souls on a regular daily basis with the manna from heaven, God's own Word of Truth. Do we realize what we are doing? Do we realize that we are standing on the lifeline; that we are an obstacle to our own spiritual life and growth?

Again we know what the Lord has to say about the privilege and the power of prayer. He says, "Whatsoever you shall ask the Father in My name, believing, you shall receive." We are encouraged, "Pray without ceasing." In one of our hymns we have the line: "Prayer is the Christian's vital breath, the Christian's native air." Prayer is like "breath" and "air" for us. When we fail to pray faithfully, we are an obstacle to ourselves. It's like standing on the oxygen line actually depriving ourselves of "vital breath"; depriving ourselves of the "abundant life" the Lord God freely offers us.

The little boy said, "I wish I'd be growed-up like my dad." When he was asked why, he replied, "Then I won't have to go to church and Sunday school anymore." See what this father was doing? By his example, he was standing on the oxygen line of his little boy. He was cutting off "vital breath." How sad, how very sad! He was a hindrance to the spiritual well-being of his own child.

Some years ago a number of college students were discussing studying the Word of God. A quick poll showed that very few of them attended a Bible study class. When I asked the reason for not "searching the Scriptures" as the Lord bids us do, I'll never forget the answer of one of the coeds: "My parents taught me not to." "What do you mean by that?" I asked. She said, "You know, actions speak louder than words. My parents never attended Bible study, so they actually taught me not to attend." I'm afraid that more often than we realize, by our poor examples, we are standing on the lifeline—cutting off "vital breath"—not only for ourselves, but also for those near and dear to us.

There are so many sin-sick people out there who are in desperate need of the Great Physician of souls, the Lord Jesus Christ. God help us to get off the oxygen line and get on with the operation that we and others, through Christ Jesus and the glorious means of grace which He has given to us and preserved for us, might not merely survive, but that we might come to possess that which our blessed Savior promises: *"I have come that you might have life, and that you might have it more abundantly"* *(John 10:10).*

Living or dying, Lord,
I ask but to be Thine;
My life in Thee, Thy life in me,
Make heav'n forever mine. Amen.

TLH 591:4

Not Today

Little girl, with shining eyes,
Her little face aglow, said,
"Daddy, it's almost time for church,
Let's go, and sing the love of Him who died
To bring us to His Father's side."

"Oh, no," said daddy, "not today,
I've worked hard all the week,
I'm going to the creek,
There I can relax the best,
I must have one day of rest
And fishing's fine, they say.
So run along, don't bother me,
I'll go to church some other day."

Now the years have passed away
And daddy hears that plea no more;
Those childish days are over.
Now that daddy's growing old
And life is almost through,
There's plenty time to go to church.
And what does daughter do?
She says, "Oh, daddy, not today,
I've stayed up most all night,
I've just got to get some sleep,
Besides, I look a fright."

Then daddy lifts a trembling hand
To brush away the tears;
Again he hears a pleading voice
Distinctly through the years.
He sees a small girl's shining face
Upturned with eyes aglow, who says:
"It's almost time for church.
Please, daddy, won't you go?"

Author Unknown

*"It's very difficult for a child to live right
if he or she has never seen it done."*

Pleasing God

The other day I was in the company of some young children who were very well schooled in saying, "please" and "thank you." What a delight! "Please, may I have more Jello?" "May I leave the table, please?" To us the word please in that sense is considered a polite request.

Then there are the words, pleased and pleasing, which carry the idea to make glad, to delight, to give satisfaction and pleasure. Pleasure is a comfortable word! We all love it! Has it ever occurred to you that we may give pleasure to God? It is recorded of the patriarch, Enoch, *"By faith Enoch was taken from this life, so that he did not experience death . . . because God had taken him away. For before he was taken, he was commended as one who PLEASED GOD"* (Heb. 11:5). Enoch, we read in Genesis 5:24, "walked with God." He was in step with God, not running ahead or lagging behind, and that PLEASED God.

Does God take pleasure in us? Do we faithfully strive to PLEASE God? In order to PLEASE God, it is necessary that we be in the right relationship with Him; that we "fear, love and trust in Him," for the Bible says, *"without faith it is impossible to PLEASE God"* (Heb. 11:6).

In this regard, what a delightful verse is *Psalm 147:11: "The Lord takes PLEASURE in them that fear Him, in those that hope in His mercy."* Fear, here, does not mean to be afraid of God. Rather, as used here, fear has the sense of respect or reverence, tenderness of feeling. In other words, because we, through the power of the Holy Spirit, love God, we fear to do the wrong.

The question is asked in Luther's Small Catechism, "When do we fear God above all things? Answer: We fear God above all things when with our whole heart we revere Him as the highest Being, honor Him with our lives, and avoid what *displeases* Him" (page 52).

In the above verse the Psalmist not only says that the Lord takes pleasure in them that "fear Him," but adds, and "those that hope in His mercy!" Those who put their future in His unfailing love, says it exactly. This is revealed so beautifully in *John 3:16: "For God so loved the world that He gave His one and only Son, that whoever believes in Him shall not perish but have eternal life."* The blessed Savior, out of mercy and love, died for our sins. *"He was wounded for our transgressions, He was bruised for our iniquities, the chastisement of our peace was upon Him, and with His stripes we are healed." (Isa. 53:5)*

Can we not lean on that love and mercy? If so, God is PLEASED. Our relationship with Him is established.

When we have been the recipients of such mercy and love, surely we would desire "to walk worthy of the Lord" as St. Paul writes to the Colossians, *"to lead a life worthy of the Lord, fully PLEASING to Him, bearing fruit in every good work and increasing in the knowledge of God" (Col. 1:10).*

Briefly summing this all up: What can we do that will be PLEASING TO GOD? It is possible to PLEASE THE LORD with our hearts and lips, with our actions, and with our possessions!

Hebrews 13:15-16: "Through Jesus, therefore, let us continually offer to God a sacrifice of praise—the fruit of lips that confess His name. And do not forget to do good and to SHARE with others, for with such sacrifices God is pleased."

The gift sent to the Apostle Paul from Philippi is called: "A sacrifice acceptable, WELL-PLEASING to God." What about our gifts to the Lord? Are they "well-pleasing" to Him?

Through the power of the Holy Spirit, may we be able to say with the Apostle Paul: *"So we make it our goal TO PLEASE THE LORD, whether we are at home in the body or away from it"* *(2 Cor. 5:9).* PLEASING GOD! Is that your goal?

What might we say of this whole matter of PLEASING GOD? One of our hymns sums it all up so beautifully, Number 529 in *The Lutheran Hymnal*:

I leave all things to God's direction,
He loveth me in weal and woe;
His will is good, true His affection,
With tender love His heart doth glow.
My Fortress and my Rock is He:
What *pleaseth* God, that *pleaseth* me.

My God hath all things in His keeping,
He is the ever faithful Friend;
He grants me laughter after weeping,
And all His ways in blessings end.
His love endures eternally:
What *pleaseth* God, that *pleaseth* me.

The will of God shall be my pleasure
While here on earth is my abode;
My will is wrong beyond all measure,
It doth not will what pleaseth God.
The Christian's motto e'er must be:
What *pleaseth* God, that *pleaseth* me.

God knows what must be done to save me,
His love for me will never cease;
Upon His hands He did engrave me
With purest gold of loving grace.
His will supreme must ever be:
What *pleaseth* God, that *pleaseth* me.

My God desires the soul's salvation,
Me also He desires to save;
Therefore with Christian resignation
All earthly troubles I will brave.
His will be done eternally:
What *pleaseth* God, that *pleaseth* me. Amen.

Let It Snow,

For a while, at least, I believe that this winter is going to be remembered in our part of the country as the winter of the big snow. One day it started snowing gently and softly. Gradually the ground was covered, and it kept on snowing. Effortlessly and silently it came and kept on coming and coming and coming.

When it was all over, factories had shut down, schools were closed, deliveries were halted. Buses were called in and travel was restricted to emergency vehicles. Everywhere one saw abandoned cars. With everything closed and all meetings cancelled, families had an unusual opportunity to get acquainted with each other again.

The reaction of people—as one might expect—varied a good deal. Those who see snow simply as something to be shoveled were irritated. There was so much of it! Others, with their cars stuck in the soft, gentle, overwhelming stuff, made the snow the object of their anger and disgust. In still others, as they watched the silent snow bring the noisy machinery of an entire city to a grinding halt, one sensed a feeling of apprehension and fear. Whatever the individual reactions, one thing was sure, everybody talked about the snow.

However, the mountains of snow offered time for reflection, and there came to mind the Bible passage: *"God . . . does great things which we cannot comprehend. For to the snow He says, 'Fall on the earth'"* *(Job 37:5,6).*

As with other things He sends, God is saying something through the snow, but it takes a listening heart to get it.

What is the message of the snow? Certainly it speaks of God's great power. He takes a snowflake, tiny, lace-like and fragile. With infinite ease He multiplies this snowflake almost endlessly and brings to a halt an entire community. The quiet power of it all shouts a warning to the unbelievers—those who deny, reject and curse Him. This God whose laws they violate and whose Word they despise; this God whom they rule out of their lives says to them, "I am still here. I have not abdicated. I am still Lord. I rule." The Psalmist quotes Him: *"Be still! And know that I am God" (Ps. 46:10).* To my knowledge there is only one place in the Bible that speaks of God laughing—"He that sits in the heavens shall laugh"—and this happens when *"The kings of the earth set themselves, and the rulers take counsel together, against the Lord, and against His Anointed, saying, Let us break their bands asunder and cast away their cords from us" (Ps. 2:2,3).* For all such who try to rule God out, the snow is the silent laughter of God.

But what about us who truly believe in the Lord God? For the Christians also the snow has a message of power; a cheering and encouraging message that this great, powerful God is on our side; for this God is our Father through Christ. We smile when little boys argue, "My dad is stronger than your dad," but their words reveal a need which we never outgrow, a need for someone bigger than we are to lean on. The God of power is our Heavenly Father, and the cold snow warms our hearts as it reminds us of this. We can always depend and lean on *Him. "Trust in the Lord with all your heart and LEAN not on your own understanding; in all your ways acknowledge Him, and He will make your paths straight."* (Prov. 3:5,6)

When, however, God says to the snow, "Be on the earth," He is also reminding us of His providential care. In the midst of the inconvenience and irritation, we do well to remember that there is good in this.

The winter wheat and our flower bulbs, rose bushes and chrysanthemums get a warm and protecting blanket; moisture is being stored in the ground against the coming drought of summer; and free of charge the soil receives a fortune in nitrogen.

Even more important in the Christian's thinking, as we listen to the message of the snow, is the snow's symbolism of God's redemptive work through His Son.

King David was looking into the clear mirror of God's Law, and what he saw was not pretty. *"I acknowledge my transgressions, and my sin is ever before me. Against Thee, Thee only, have I sinned and done this evil in Thy sight."* (Ps. 51:3f.) In nine verses he uses the words transgression, iniquity and sin ten times. And then comes the note of hope, "Wash me, and I shall be WHITER THAN SNOW."

In another place God is speaking, and He uses the same picture. *"Come now, and let us reason together, saith the Lord. Though your sins be as scarlet, THEY SHALL BE AS WHITE AS SNOW."* (Isa. 1:18) How beautiful, comforting and soul-strengthening are confession, repentance and absolution!

The snow, before the soot and dirt spoil it, has an incredible whiteness. But David says, "whiter than snow." The whitest thing in all of nature is insufficient to portray the cleansing job God performs on us through the precious blood of His Son. When God gives us the grace to see the crushing blackness of our sins, we can confidently sing—and the snow reminds us of this—"Wash me, and I SHALL BE WHITER THAN SNOW."

The blood of God's Son, our Savior, is the only known sin remover. It is yours and mine free of charge, a gift of love of which we pray, praise and give thanks saying and singing:

Lord, to you I make confession:
I have sinned and gone astray,
I have multiplied transgression,
Chosen for myself my way.
Led by you to see my errors,
Lord, I tremble at your terrors.

Though my conscience' voice appall me,
Father, I will seek your face;
Though your child I dare not call me,
Yet receive me in your grace.
Do not for my sins forsake me;
Let your wrath not overtake me.

Your Son came to suffer for me,
Gave himself to rescue me,
Died to heal me and restore me,
Reconciled and set me free.
Jesus' cross alone can vanquish
These dark fears and soothe this anguish.
Lord, on you I cast my burden.

Sink it to the depths below.
Let me know your gracious pardon,
WASH ME, MAKE ME WHITE AS SNOW.
Let your Spirit leave me never;
Make me only yours forever.

LW 233:1-4

Conviction, Conversion, Confession

The Rev. T. A. Raedeke once challenged his audience to present God's plan of salvation in ten words or less. Perhaps most of us immediately thought of John 3:16. While God's plan of salvation is clearly outlined in that passage, the passage contains 25 words.

Pastor Raedeke went on to tell about Bishop Taylor, one of the chief of chaplains in the English army during the First World War who applied a simple test to all British ministers who volunteered to serve as army chaplains during the conflict.

With his open watch in his hand, the Bishop would say to each applicant: "I am a dying soldier. I have only one minute to live. Tell me what I must do to be saved." If the prospective chaplain answered within that minute, *"Believe in the Lord Jesus Christ, and you will be saved" (Acts 16:31),* or words to that effect, he was admitted. If he gave any other answer, he was rejected.

Dr. Raedeke suggested that if we were limited to ten words in presenting Gods plan of salvation, we could use these six words, "Believe in the Lord Jesus Christ." However, some people with analytical minds might not be satisfied with that answer. They might ask: "What does it mean to believe; what does belief imply?" So to satisfy these people we might add four more words—"Remember the penitent thief." The penitent thief not only showed what it means to believe, but he clearly demonstrates the three basic elements necessary for faith and salvation. These three basic elements are: CONVICTION, CONVERSION AND CONFESSION.

CONVICTION is the sinners attitude toward himself; CONVERSION is the sinners attitude toward Christ; CONFESSION is the sinners attitude toward his fellow sinners for whom Christ also died.

Salvation without CONVICTION is an impossibility. Before we can be saved for something we must be saved from something. If we say we have no sin, we will feel no need of salvation. The penitent malefactor was CONVICTED on account of his sin. Listen to his words, *"We receive the due rewards of our deed" (Luke 23:41).* He was terrified because of his sin. He feared and felt the judgment of God. Listen as he rebukes the impenitent malefactor, *"Do you not fear God, seeing that we are in the same condemnation?" (Luke 23:40).* This man was CONVICTED of his sin.

If we think lightly of sin, we may not have experienced the Savior's promise that the Holy Spirit would CONVICT us of our sins. Unless we have this CONVICTION, we will feel no need of a Savior. Jesus said, *"I have not come to call the righteous, but sinners to REPENTANCE. Those who are well have no need of a physician, but those who are sick" (Mark 2:17).*

However, being CONVICTED of sin is not enough. A CONVICTED sinner is doomed and damned because he sees only himself and his sins.

The more he sees of himself, the further he is driven from God. Therefore, the second element of faith is necessary, namely, CONVERSION.

A CONVERTED sinner takes his eyes off himself, and in the strength of the Holy Spirit, fastens them on Christ as his only hope and his only help. Instead of running away from God, the CONVERTED sinner is turned around and fastens his eyes and heart on God. This CONVERSION, this turning around, is the sole work of the Holy Spirit.

Judas betrayed his Lord for 30 pieces of silver. Judas was CONVICTED of his sin. Judas left Jesus. He went out into the night; he despaired. Peter denied Jesus three times. The Lord looked at Peter, and Peter was CONVICTED of sin; he went out and wept bitterly. But he remembered that look of Jesus, and he continued to look to Jesus for forgiveness. Jesus not only warned him of his sin but had told him in advance: *"When you are CONVICTED, strengthen your brethren"* (Luke 22:32).

CONVICTION and CONVERSION—but still no salvation! Is it possible to be saved and enter the realm of saints without CONFESSING Christ? Regardless of what we may think, the Bible says in Romans 10:9f., clearly and unmistakably: *"If you CONFESS with your lips that Jesus is Lord and believe in your heart that God raised Him from the dead, you will be saved. For man believes with his heart and so is justified, and he CONFESSES with his lips and so is saved."*

Take another look at the penitent thief and hear his CONFESSION, *"We receive the due rewards of our deeds"* (Luke 23:41). We certainly would never have faulted him if he had not witnessed to the other malefactor. We may not even have noticed it.

When did we, you and I, last CONFESS Jesus Christ as our personal sin-atoning Savior? The great sin of omission of the Christian Church today and of Christians in particular is that we fail to share Christ. Consequently

178

the Christian Church is growing, but proportionately growing smaller. The birth rate by far exceeds the re-birth rate.

Ten words with a glorious message for all: "Believe in the Lord Jesus Christ . . . Remember the penitent thief." What, now, is OUR GLORIOUS TASK? Here it is:

Hark, the voice of Jesus calling,
  "Who will go and work today?
Fields are white and harvests waiting,
  Who will bear the sheaves away?"
Loud and long the master calls you;
  Rich reward he offers free.
Who will answer, gladly saying,
  "Here am I. Send me, send me."?

If you cannot speak like angels,
  If you cannot preach like Paul,
You can tell the love of Jesus;
  You can say he died for all.
If you cannot rouse the wicked
  With the judgment's dread alarms,
You can lead the little children
  To the Savior's waiting arms.

If you cannot be a watchman,
  Standing high on Zion's wall,
Pointing out the path to heaven,
  Off'ring life and peace to all,
With your prayers and with your bounties
  You can do what God demands;
You can be like faithful Aaron,
  Holding up the prophet's hands.

Let none hear you idly saying,
  "There is nothing I can do,"
While the multitudes are dying
  And the master calls for you.
Take the task he gives you gladly;
  Let his work your pleasure be.
Answer quickly when he calls you,
  "Here am I. Send me, send me."

LW 318

With whom will you be sharing these important ten words: "REMEMBER THE PENITENT THIEF. BELIEVE ON THE LORD JESUS CHRIST" ??

The Old Porch Swing

About forty years ago I visited an old, venerable pastor and his dear wife. They were enjoying one of their favorite pastimes, swinging back and forth in the old swing on the back porch. The pastor and his wife loved that old swing. "Mom and I don't get very far in this thing," the old pastor said, "but here's where we reminisce and also solve many of our problems." And then Mom chimed in, "And here's where we count our blessings. Oh, we have so very much for which to be thankful! Our dear Lord has been so good to us!" Oh, yes, many precious moments were spent on the old swing chained firmly to the rafters of the back porch.

Can we, believers in the Lord Jesus Christ, find a message in an old porch swing? I believe that we can. Back and forth it moves—always moving, but really getting no place. Are we, like that old porch swing, moving back and forth, back and forth, and yet never really getting anywhere? Perhaps so. We swing forth with dreams, plans, thoughts, ideas and resolves. For example, we plan to have daily family devotions. We have ideas about reaching out to new neighbors and new members. We think and talk about how important it is to witness our faith. We want to share God's love, forgiveness and salvation. We resolve to follow a daily Bible reading plan. We promise ourselves that we are going to be more fervent and diligent in our prayer life. But—just like that old porch swing—so often we find ourselves stuck, anchored and chained fast—swinging forward but then back again, making no real advances—going nowhere.

But wait a minute! That old swing may be chained fast, but we are not! Once we were, of course, but now we're not! We're free! Did you get that? We are free! Christ Jesus broke the chains that bound us when on the cross He paid our price—freeing us to go forth, to do, to move ahead, to grow, to progress. Remember, *"If the Son makes you free, you will be free indeed" (John 8:36).* Oh, yes, Christ Jesus frees us so that now we can live to Him, with Him and for Him and *"we can do all things through Him who strengthens us" (Phil. 4:13). "If you continue in My Word,"* Jesus declares, *"you are truly My disciples, and you will know the Truth, and the Truth will make you free" (John 8:32).* No one knew that better than the sainted pastor and his wife, Pop and Mom Wambsganss. A little song of praise says it this way:

Freely, freely, you have received
Freely, freely give.
Go in My name, and because you believe,
Others will know that I live.

We pray:
Oh, may this bounteous God
Thro' all our life be near us,
With ever joyful hearts
And blessed peace to cheer us
And keep us in His grace
And guide us when perplexed
AND FREE US FROM ALL ILLS
In this world and the next!

TLH 36:2

"When we depend on man, we get what man can do; when we depend on prayer, we get what God can do."

The Known Unknown

Does the heading sound contradictory?
Let me explain.

The other day I heard some folks talking about the New Year and its unknowns, its uncertainties. One said, "We really don't have an idea what's in store for us." "Yeah," said another, "the future is really hidden from us." "All, all is so uncertain," chimed in another. "We just don't know. It's really like being in the dark."

We don't know? Like being in the dark? No idea what's in store for us? Everything is hidden from us? All is uncertain? Now, just what kind of talk is that?

For the child of God facing a new year of grace means stepping into the future that has almost limitless certainties. It is one of the thrilling realities of the Christian hope (future) that what may be unknown and uncertain to us is known and certain to our God who has promised to give us all that we need to face the future with courage and confidence.

He has said, for example, that "nothing," get that, *"nothing shall be able to separate us from the LOVE OF GOD IN CHRIST JESUS, our Lord"* (Rom. 8:39).

Nothing shall be able to separate us from the love of God in the New Year or any time in the future. What more security do we want or need than that promise of our God? Talk about certainty! Talk about what's in store for us! Talk about being in the know, about walking in the light!

Furthermore, our Lord has assured us that He will be with us always, *"even to the end of the age" (Matt. 28:20).* Talk about certainty in the future! To be with us to the end! That's a long-range social security program if I have ever heard of one. And we can be sure of it. It's certain. God, our God says so!

You say you will have many needs in the new year. Why not put your heart and your future on deposit with the Lord God, even as St. Paul did when he wrote: *"My God shall supply all your need according to His riches in glory by Christ Jesus"* (Phil. 4:19). ALL your need! Get that? What a blank check signed by our living Lord!

There are so many certainties in the uncertain. There are so many knowns in the unknown. Search them out. Take hold of them with the hand of faith. Ponder them. Believe them. Cling to them. Apply them. Don't let anyone or anything wrest them from you.

And remember, God's love for us cannot and will not diminish as our years pass and our strength and our resources diminish. St. Paul's logical hope was: *"He that spared not His own Son, but delivered HIM UP FOR US ALL, how shall He not with Him also freely give us ALL THINGS?"* (Rom. 8:32). What amazing grace! What blessed assurance!

Watch for the fulfillment of these certainties, these knowns in the coming year and in the rest of your days! We know by faith that they are true. Believing is seeing! God's promises are dependable. We can count on them.

Let each day that the Lord gives be a waiting on Him for their unfolding. Lord, Oh Lord, be with us yet lest we forget, lest we forget!

Our God, our Help in ages past,
Our Hope for years to come,
Be Thou our Guard while troubles last
And our eternal Home! Amen.

TLH 123:8

Be Ready to Resign

There was this town's so-called "no good" who, one evening, wandered into a church meeting and was captivated by the energetic and appealing message of the preacher. He felt the tug of the message, but warily endeavored to remain dispassionate about the whole thing. All around him were people who were succumbing with "Amens." Finally, swept away by his emotions, he called out: "Use me, Lord, use me, BUT ONLY IN AN ADVISORY CAPACITY!"

All of us are engaged in "church work," serving on boards, committees, filling this position or that. Whether you were elected, appointed, assigned, whether you volunteered, were "called" or plain "roped in," just because it is church work doesn't mean that everything goes smoothly all the time.

All of you know that, at times, there are struggles, disappointments, irritations and frustrations. At times we experience some real let-downs and defeats.

Fortunately for you, I have the answer to all of this. I have the solution. Other than serving only in an advisory capacity, there is a way to get around all of this. Actually it is following a very simple rule.

Over the years I have found it never to fail. I don't know if all of you are really ready for this, but here it is: Whenever you encounter difficulties or obstacles of any kind, just follow this simple rule: I call it BRTR. It stands for: **BE READY TO RESIGN.**

When you don't get the full cooperation from everyone, **BRTR.**

When unexpected difficulties loom before you:
BE READY TO RESIGN.
When the task becomes increasingly more difficult:
BRTR.
When things go wrong (which most of the time simply means that others are not proceeding according to your plan):
BE READY TO RESIGN.
When it appears that your efforts aren't being appreciated, and that you are obviously being taken advantage of:
BRTR.
When you find yourself going in circles (not only big wheels, but also little ones go that way, you know):
BE READY TO RESIGN.
When you are convinced that there is no way that everything is actually going to come out ok: *BRTR.*

When, according to your calculations and schedule, you don't see sufficient progress:
BE READY TO RESIGN.
When it appears that your talent and your experience aren't being given proper consideration:
BRTR.
Oh, yes, and when you get your feelings hurt:
BE READY TO RESIGN.
That is my simple rule: *BE READY TO RESIGN,*
BRTR.

No, I don't mean resign from your position or your committee or board or whatever. I don't mean quit your task and run away from the challenges and opportunities. Rather, I mean *RESIGN YOURSELF TO YOUR LORD AND TO HIS GOOD AND GRACIOUS WILL.*

Inspired by God, Isaiah of old has something very special for us. He asks: *"Have you not known? Have you not heard?"* Or, have you forgotten? *"The Lord is the everlasting God, the Creator of the ends of the earth. He does not faint or grow weary, His understanding is unreachable. He gives power to the faint, and to him who has no might He increases strength. Even youths shall faint and be weary, and young men shall fall exhausted; but they who wait for the Lord shall renew their strength, they shall mount up with wings like eagles, they shall run and not be weary, they shall walk and not faint"* (Isa. 40:28-31).

And then the Lord God, through His man Isaiah, goes on to remind us: *"You are My servant, I have chosen you and not cast you off; fear not, for I am with you, be not dismayed, for I am your God; I will strengthen you, I will help you, I will uphold you with My victorious hand"* (Isa. 41:10).

You see, there is really only one thing for us to do. **LORD, I RESIGN . . . . myself to YOU!**

My Jesus, as You will;
Oh, may Your will be mine!
Into Your hand of love
I WOULD MY ALL RESIGN.
Thro' sorrow or thro' joy
Conduct me as Your own
And help me still to say,
Your will be done.

O Lord divine,
My heart and all
I now resign . . . TO YOU!

The Bottle

"No deposit—no return"!
That's what it said on
the bottle that I found.

No one wants it anymore.
It's not good for a thing anymore.
"Throw it away! It has
lived its usefulness."

"No deposit—no return."
Thank God, He doesn't stamp
us with that phrase.

Maybe we should stop trying
to stamp each other!

Ministers—The Congregation

Some time ago I received a Sunday church bulletin that listed the names of those participating. There was the name of the pastor, the organist, song leader, bell ringer, acolytes and the liturgist. Above all these was printed: MINISTERS—ALL MEMBERS OF THE CONGREGATION.

Being intrigued by the word, MINISTERS, being used as the members of the congregation, I decided to check on its origin. In my 17 pound, 3,350 page *Webster International Dictionary* I read the following under the word MINISTER:

> From the root word of minor; a servant, and attendant; one who waits upon or ministers to others; to perform services; to do things needful or helpful; to render aid; to be serviceable; to be subordinate; to comply with commands or demands; one who acts under the orders of another.

And then in my dictionary these words of our blessed Savior follow:

> "... *whosoever will be great among you, let him be your minister; and whosoever will be chief among you, let him be your servant: Even as the Son of man came not to be ministered unto, but to minister, and to give His life as a ransom for many*" (Matt. 28:26-28).

What a beautiful, weekly reminder for the members of that congregation! And how all of us need that reminder that we, by the grace and mercy of God, are to be ministers to others—waiting upon, reaching out to, and by love serving one another! We are servants, saved to serve! Ministers! Servants!

The word "servant" (*doulos*) is found about 120 times in the New Testament. However, the implications of *doulos* go deeper. Actually it means "bond-servant" or "slave." The title certainly offers no glamour, no source of earthly pride. And yet, Jesus proclaimed the *"doulos"* principle as the *gateway to greatness*!

And yet to us a bond-servant or slave and greatness don't seem to go together at all! According to human standards the great are those who wield power, hold positions of authority; those who possess special leadership qualities. Even in religious circles, the "great" are often those who are especially gifted, the ones with charisma, the powerful, persuasive; the ones bestowed with degrees of honor.

However, Jesus, God's Son and our Savior, never endorsed such a standard. In Mark 10:35ff. He emphasized His viewpoint of true greatness when James and John asked Him for a place of honor in His kingdom. He pointed out how the world evaluates greatness, and then He said, *"So shall it NOT be among you."*

Jesus, then, goes on to state the principle by which He determines greatness when He declares: *"Whoever would be first among you must be slave (doulos) of all"* (Mark 10:44). And then He follows up by declaring: *"For the Son of man also came not to be served BUT TO SERVE, and to give His life as a ransom for many"* (Mark 10:45). Jesus was the highest—in the form of God. Then

He became the lowest—in the form of a slave.

If we want a clear picture as to what this meant to Christ, we go to the Upper Room and the Last Supper. Hear the disciples as they argue about who would be greatest. Then watch Jesus as He takes a bowl of water and a *"doulos"* towel, and performs the task usually performed by the slaves in the household—washing the feet of the guests.

And notice whose feet Jesus washes. The feet of Peter, though He knew Peter would shortly deny Him, one, two, three times! The feet of Thomas, who would doubt Him. The feet of Judas who would betray Him for a few pieces of silver, and the feet of the rest of the disciples even though He knew all of them would forsake Him in His great hour of need. What a lesson for us! That was the *"doulos"* principle in its purest form! Why did Jesus do it? Jesus gave the answer Himself, recorded in *John 13:12-17:*

"When He had washed their feet, and taken His garments, and resumed His place, He said to them, "Do you know what I have done to you? You call me Teacher and Lord; and you are right, for so I am. If then I, your Lord and Teacher, have washed your feet, you also ought to wash one another's feet. For I have given you an example, that you also should do as I have done to you. Truly, truly, I say to you, a servant (doulos) is not greater than his master; nor is he who is sent greater than he who sent him. If you know these things, blessed are you if you do them."

What an example the Lord gives all of us when it comes to serving others, when it comes to being *ministers*! What a difference the *"doulos* principle" could make! How much different it would be in our homes, our churches, schools, neighborhoods, work places and our nation, if we would adopt THE *DOULOS* PRINCIPLE as the guiding rule for our lives! Yes, "by love serve one another!" In other words, "we have been saved to serve," to *minister, minister*!

Each of us can make a difference by becoming, in the strength of the Lord, a true *minister,* a bond-servant of Jesus. Are you a bond-servant of Jesus Christ?

St. Paul liked to call himself that, a bond-servant. It meant more than "servant" or "slave" of Jesus Christ. According to Exodus 21, a purchased Hebrew slave was entitled to his freedom the seventh year, after serving six years. However, he could elect to remain as a slave rather than leave the master whom he had grown to love and who had cared for him lovingly. He could say, "I love my master. I will not go out free. I will serve him all the days of my life."

His master would, then, bring him to the authorities and the master, we read, would "bore his ear through with an awl." This would mark him as a "bond-servant" who had chosen to serve his master voluntarily for the rest of his days. What about us who have been saved solely by grace through faith in Christ Jesus? What is our response to the free gift of eternal life? The Scriptures remind us: *"It is God Himself who has made us what we are and has given us new lives from Christ Jesus; and long ages ago He planned that we should spend these lives in helping, serving, ministering to others" (Eph. 2:10).*

Let's go back to that statement in that bulletin: MINISTERS—THE CONGREGATION. Out of love and gratitude to our precious Savior for what He has done for us, and out of love for our fellowman, would you be a MINISTER of His the rest of your days?

Here and now, make this your plea and pledge:

God of grace and love and blessing,
Thine alone shall be the praise;
Give us hearts to trust Thee truly,
Hands to serve Thee all our days.
Lord, bestow Thy future blessing
Till we join the heav'nly host,
There to praise and serve Thee ever,
Father, Son, and Holy Ghost. Amen.

TLH 640:4

What Work Do You Do for the Lord?

A housewife was once approached by an active church member and asked: "And what work do you do for the Lord?" Her reply was simple and direct, "ALL OF IT!"

There was perhaps more good theology in those three words than in any other answer the woman could have given. ALL of her work was being done for the Lord! While it was no doubt true that some of her deeds were more directly in the service of the Lord than others, she still felt that EVERYTHING she did was in the service of her Lord and Master.

There is a lesson for all of us in the simple answer of this humble wife and mother. In a day when we are inclined to draw too sharp a line between the sacred and the secular, there is an ever-present danger that we draw an artificial distinction between what we do for the Lord through the organizational channels of the church and what we do for Him in the humdrum routine of our everyday life. By inspiration the Apostle Paul writes; *"Whatever your task, work heartily, as serving the Lord"* (Col. 3:23).

The Christian serves the Lord Christ in every station of life—as father, mother, etc. Whatever our calling, if it is to the glory of God and the welfare of our fellowman, we can discharge our daily duties "as serving the Lord."

That is what the busy wife and mother meant when she replied to the question, "And what work do you do for the Lord?" by saying: "All of it!" There was nothing that she was not doing for the Lord. Can we say the same?

- *Excerpts from an article by*
Herman W. Gockel

Dear Lord Jesus, every task be to You commended;
May Your will be done, I ask, until life is ended.
Jesus, in Your name begun be the day's endeavor;
Grant that it may well be done to Your praise forever.

Amen.

- Adapted

Remember and Forget Not

Most of us would like to have a better memory. Life would be easier, and even more exciting, if we could remember people we have met, things we have heard and even what we have to do. Students need class schedules, teachers need record books, business people need desk calendars and we all need daily reminders at home to keep us on schedule.

Not everything, of course, is important enough to remember, but some things are far too important to forget. As Christians we can so easily pray, promising the Lord that we will give Him the praise, honor and glory when the answer comes, only to forget that promise all too soon.

Sooner or later crises of various kinds confront us all. In those times we find the Lord to be our Strength, our Comfort and our Guide. At the time we are certain that we will ever be grateful to Him for bringing us through. But, then, all too soon we forget. How we all need to be reminded and encouraged: REMEMBER AND FORGET NOT!

Note just a few pertinent passages from the Scriptures:

✝ *"Remember and forget not
   the Lord your God."* (Deut. 8:18)

✝ *"Remember the sabbath day,
   to keep it holy."* (Ex. 20:8)

✝ *"Do not forget the works of God,*
  but keep His commandments." (Ps. 78:7)

✝ *"All the ends of the earth shall remember and turn to*
  the Lord; and all the families of the nations shall
  worship before Him." (Ps. 22:27)

✝ *"Remember the wonderful works*
  the Lord has done." (Ps. 105:5)

✝ *"Bless the Lord, O my soul,*
  and forget not all His benefits,
  who forgives all your iniquity,
  who heals all your diseases,
  who redeems your life from the Pit,
  who crowns you with steadfast love and mercy,
  who satisfies you with good as long as you live."

(Ps. 102:3f.)

Oh, yes, REMEMBER AND FORGET NOT!

When Joshua led the people of Israel across the Jordan River into the promised land, God instructed him to have one man from each tribe take a stone from the very spot in the midst of the River Jordan where the priests stood firm on dry land while the people passed over. The twelve stones were carried to the Gilgal side, and there Joshua set them up as a memorial to the mercy of God (Note Joshua, chapter 4).

The reason was clear. They were NEVER TO FORGET the miracle of God in their hour of crisis. They could always be encouraged in every situation of life BY REMEMBERING how God had intervened in a time of great distress, and then were commanded to give their testimony to their children when they would see those stones and ask: "What do these stones mean?"

While we today would not employ the same method to remind us of the mercies of God, we need to do whatever is necessary, for us, to always REMEMBER God's faithfulness and love and to share our experiences with others. Perhaps we need to set up our own "stones" to REMEMBER AND FORGET NOT!

Let mercy cause me to be willing
To bear my lot and not to fret.
While He my restless heart is stilling,
May I His mercy NOT FORGET!
Come weal, come woe, my heart to test,
His mercy is my only rest.

I Have No Man

There is a Biblical account of someone who said to Jesus, "I HAVE NO MAN." Actually, it is a very sad scene. Can you recall it? Do you know who uttered these words to Jesus, "I HAVE NO MAN"? You are familiar with the story, I am quite certain. However, since I have lifted these four words from the account, it might be a little difficult for you to properly place them.

The Apostle John writes about this, chapter 5, verses 1-7. *"I HAVE NO MAN"* was the cry of the helpless cripple at the Pool of Bethesda. When our Lord asked him, *"Do you want to be healed?"* the helpless, crippled man answered, *"I HAVE NO MAN, when the water is troubled, to put me into the pool."*

This man at the Pool of Bethesda is a pretty good picture of all mankind by nature. By nature all of us are impotent, crippled and helpless. By nature, the Bible says, "we are blind, dead and enemies of God."

However, in your case and mine someone—a father, a mother, a Sunday school teacher, a friend, a pastor—someone at some time said to us: "BEHOLD THE MAN!" In other words, someone bore witness to Jesus. Someone led us to Christ the God Man. Someone told us of Jesus and His love, His forgiveness, and His salvation. When we HAD NO MAN, someone said, "There is help, there is hope, there is forgiveness and salvation for you. There is heaven. BEHOLD THE MAN!"

By God's abundant grace, and because someone was faithful in sharing Christ, in pointing to Him and saying,

"BEHOLD THE MAN!" here we are, His own, living in His kingdom of grace and looking forward to His kingdom of glory.

At all times, but especially during the season of Lent we "BEHOLD THE MAN"; we "Behold the Lamb of God who takes away the sin of the world," pleading for His mercy.

But let us remember, while we are doing that—and rejoicing in it—there are millions upon millions for whom He died who are still crying out: "I HAVE NO MAN!"

Who are these? They could be the people living across the street from you, or someone with whom you ride to work, someone with whom you work. Could be your mailman or a customer of yours. Could be someone living under the same roof with you; someone with the same last name as you. These are like the helpless cripple at the Pool of Bethesda. THEY HAVE NO MAN!

Just think of it, you have what they need! Rather, you have WHOM they need! Go to them, speak to them, urge them, lead them to BEHOLD THE MAN! The Lord is counting on you and me to bring them to Him. He will heal them even as He did that one who, long ago, said, "I HAVE NO MAN." We are told, "Jesus said to him, 'Rise, take up your cot and walk.' And at once the man was healed, and he took up his cot and walked."

BEHOLD THE MAN! To whom could you say that? To your mate, your children, a brother or a sister, perhaps a neighbor?

Parable of a Neighbor

A certain family moved into our community and didn't fall among thieves—they just moved in. A neighbor came by and saw them but decided, "I'm running late today; besides the pastor probably knows about them." Another neighbor came by; he thought, "I'm not a fanatic about religion; I'll wait until they bring it up, then invite them to church." Another neighbor came by, stopped and welcomed them to the community. He showed interest in their spiritual life and invited them to church. He even offered to come by for them and did. He helped the children enroll in Sunday school and assisted in any way he could.

Now, which of these do you think was neighbor unto those who moved to the community?

Go and do thou likewise!

What Would He Say?

If He should come today
And find my hands so full
Of future plans, however fair,
In which my Savior had no share,
What would He say?

If He should come today
And find I had not told
One soul about my heavenly Friend,
Whose blessings all my way attend,
What would He say?

If He should come today,
Would I be glad, quite glad?
Remembering He had died for all,
And none through me had heard His call,
What would I say?

How Are You?

When asked "How are you?", my grandmother would frequently answer: "I'm mostly alright." When I am greeted with the question, "How are you?" invariably I will answer, "I am grateful!" Usually people will say, "Oh, that's a good answer. We all have so very much for which to be grateful." And then I can ask, "For what especially are you grateful at this particular time?" What a great way to get a conversation going—talking, praising and thanking the Lord for special gifts that we have received from His loving hands!

When John Quincy Adams was an old man he was met one day by a friend who greeted him with those familiar words: "How are you, Mr. Adams?" The elderly Adams replied, "John Quincy Adams himself is very well, thank you, but the old house in which he lives is falling to pieces. Time and the seasons have nearly destroyed it. I think John Quincy Adams will soon have to move out. But he himself is very well, sir."

Mr. Adams was, of course, referring to his aging body as "the old house" on which the passing years had taken their toll and from which his immortal soul would soon have to take its leave.

The Apostle Paul put it this way: *"Do not lose heart. Though our outer nature (body) is wasting away, our inner nature (soul) is being refreshed and renewed every day. For this slight momentary affliction is preparing for us an eternal weight of glory beyond all comparison, because we look not to the things that are seen but to the things that are unseen; for the things that are seen are transient, but the things that are unseen are eternal"* (2 Cor. 4:16f.).

For the people of God there is really no dread in the rapid flight of time. The passing years may bring with them their multiplied reminders that "swift to its close ebbs out life's little day" when we experience waning strength, fading vigor, the slowing step, the blurring vision, the aching joints, the increasing forgetfulness, etc., but we are also reminded of the glorious assurances by which our "inward man" (eternal soul) is renewed day after day.

How avidly the "inward man" of the maturing Christian feeds upon the precious Gospel promises! With each passing year these promises of our precious Savior mean more and more to us. With each passing year—and I write from experience—these promises of God pour new strength, new joy, new hope into our souls.

How could it be otherwise? If God's promises are true—and in Christ all of His promises are "Yea and Amen," or in other words, *"All the promises of God find their Yes in Him" (1 Cor. 1:20)*—then every passing day, week, month and year bring us that much nearer to the complete fulfillment of all God's promises to us. Without question, "a heap of living" has its very special blessings.

The new, young pastor called on an elderly couple. After he left the wife said to her aged husband, "Isn't he a fine young man? And wasn't that a wonderful devotion he had for us?" The old gentleman responded, "Yes, he certainly is a fine young man, but he will have to do 'a heap of living' before he can fully understand what he shared with us in the Scriptures." Oh, yes, the inspired Word of our God keeps unfolding!

He who fulfilled His ancient pledges by the miracles of Bethlehem, Jerusalem, Gethsemane and Calvary, and also Joseph's Garden, will surely keep His promise to come again and to take us to Himself to the eternal mansions on high that He has gone to prepare for us. Each day that we put behind us is another day that we have traveled closer to our Father's house where we will experience *"fullness of joy, and at His right hand, pleasures forevermore"* *(Ps. 16:11).*

Isn't it a wonder that the believing people of God can say with the Apostle Paul, *"Though our outward man perish, yet the inward man is renewed day by day"* *(2 Cor. 4:16).* For it is the inward man that is daily feeding on the refreshing manna of the promises of heaven. And it is of heaven, which is ours solely by grace through faith in Christ Jesus, of which we love to sing:

I'm but a stranger here,
Heav'n is my home;
Earth is a desert drear,
Heav'n is my home.
Danger and sorrow stand
Round me on ev'ry hand;
Heav'n is my fatherland,
Heav'n is my home.

What though the tempest rage,
Heav'n is my home;
Short is my pilgrimage,
Heav'n is my home;
And time's wild wintry blast
Soon shall be over-past;
I shall reach home at last,
Heav'n is my home.

There at my Savior's side
Heav'n is my home;
I shall be glorified,
Heav'n is my home.
There are the good and blest,
Those I love most and best;
And there I, too, shall rest,
Heav'n is my home.

Therefore I murmur not,
Heav'n is my home;
Whate'er my earthly lot,
Heav'n is my home;
And I shall surely stand
There at my Lord's right hand.
Heav'n is my fatherland,
Heav'n is my home. Amen.

TLH 660

A Mighty Leading
and Deliverance

I believe that the third and fourth chapters of Exodus certainly must be one of the most fascinating portions of the whole Old Testament. These two chapters, you will recall, tell how God calls Moses to lead His people out of what had become terrible slavery in Egypt.

Moses, a fugitive from Egyptian authorities, had settled down in Midian. There he was tending the flock of his father-in-law, Jethro. On this occasion he has brought his flock to Horeb, "the Mountain of God." He notices a strange phenomenon. A flame of fire is burning a bush, but the bush is not consumed. It keeps on burning.

Intrigued, Moses says to himself: "I will turn aside and see this great sight, why the bush is not burnt." That's when God calls to Moses, tells him to take off his shoes (because he is standing on holy ground), and informs Moses that He, God, is talking. Moses hides his face. He is afraid to look at holy God. I would have been afraid— and perhaps you would have been afraid, too.

God tells Moses that He has heard the anguished praying of His people in Egypt. He will deliver them and bring them to a good land, one "flowing with milk and honey." And, God adds, "I will send YOU to Pharaoh that YOU may bring forth My people."

Moses is stunned. He asks, "Who am I, that I should go to Pharaoh?" God says, "I will be with you."

Moses wonders about the people of Israel accepting him. What if they ask who has sent him? "What shall I say to them?" God replies: "Say this . . . the Lord . . . has sent me to you . . ."

Moses isn't convinced. "They will not believe me," he tells God. Patiently God strengthens Moses' shaky faith. Throw your rod on the ground, God tells the hesitating shepherd. Moses does, and the rod turns into a serpent, big and dangerous enough so that Moses flees from it. And now a bit of a test of obedience, for God instructs Moses: "Take it by the tail!" I don't know how eagerly Moses obeyed, but he did do it, and the serpent again becomes a rod.

Then God tells him to put his hand inside his cloak. When he takes it out it is white with the terrible disease of leprosy. When Moses repeats the process the hand returns to normal. By these signs, God tells him, the people will believe you.

Moses still isn't ready. "Oh, my Lord," he says, "I am not eloquent . . . " To which the Lord God responds: "Who has made man's mouth? Go, and I will be with your mouth and teach you what you shall speak."

Once more Moses tries to avoid the call of the Lord. He has used up all his excuses. Now he simply pleads, "Oh my Lord, send, I pray, some other person." Now God becomes a little angry at his hesitant prophet. Still God is patient. He arranges for Moses' brother, Aaron, to be Moses' spokesman. This satisfies Moses. He takes his leave from Jethro, and with his wife and sons heads out for Egypt. And we read, "In his hand Moses took THE ROD OF GOD."

Here is an account just loaded with helpful and encouraging insights and instructions for us. How patient

God is with us! He meets Moses' foot-dragging objections one by one until the shepherd is ready to function as the prophet called by his Lord.

What an encouragement for us to talk to God, and to keep talking to Him! How good of the Lord to let us experience the "burning bushes" of Holy Baptism, Holy Communion and the Holy Scriptures!

Most of all let us, as have His people down through the ages, see in this inspired and inspiring account a picture of what would happen 1500 years later at another mountain of God called Calvary.

You and I, with all people, were cursed with a most terrible bondage, the bondage of sin. We were utter slaves with no hope of helping ourselves even a little. Only the Lord God could bring us out of that deadly slavery into the promised land of forgiveness, life and eternal salvation.

God HAS delivered us. He HAS set us free. He sent us the Greater Moses, His Son, Jesus. He sent Him to Mt. Calvary, "Calvary's mournful mountain." The Greater Shepherd loaded down with all OUR guilt and shame paid the price required to "free us from all guilt in this world and the next." By His stripes we are healed! We are free! In Jesus we are free!

And in that blessed freedom we, like Moses, and under God's patient caring and calling, become His sent ones. "As My Father sent Me," Jesus says, "so send I you." What will we say to all of this?

Let none hear you idly saying,
"There is nothing I can do,"
While the souls of men are dying
And the Master calls for you.
Take the task He gives you gladly,
Let His work your pleasure be;
Answer quickly when He calleth,
"Here am I, send me, send me!" Amen.

TLH 496:4

The Power of Words

A careless word may kindle strife;
A cruel word may wreck a life.
A bitter word may hate instill;
A brutal word may smite and kill.
A gracious word may smooth the way;
A joyous word may light the day.
A timely word may lessen stress;
A loving word may heal and bless.

What If?

(1 Cor. 15:14, 17, 18, 20)

"WHAT IF?"
"What if?" What a world of meaning is in these words!
What if -
we didn't have enough water to drink?
What if -
we didn't have enough food to eat?
What if -
a tornado would pass through our town?
What if -
there were a nuclear war?
What if -
you were told you had an incurable disease?
What if - we didn't have freedom of religion?

What if? What if? What if?

The Apostle Paul poses a "What if" question in his first letter to the Corinthians, the fifteenth chapter:

WHAT IF Jesus had not risen from the dead? He then contemplates the horrible consequences:
1. *"Our preaching is in vain."* v. 14
Our preaching, teaching, witnessing, our establishing new congregations, supporting seminaries—if Jesus had not risen from the dead—all would be in vain, foolish, folly, worthless, useless. After all, why preach and teach and witness about a dead Christ?

214

BUT HALLELUJAH! All our preaching and teaching and living is centered around the RISEN LORD JESUS! The Bible declares, *"This Jesus God raised up, and of that we are all witnesses" (Acts 2:32).*

Again, we ask, WHAT IF Jesus had not risen from the dead? WHAT IF? And Paul says:

2. *"Your faith is vain."* v. 14

If Christ is not risen, it is not only folly to preach and to teach about a dead person, but foolish to believe in one. Paul says, then "your faith is vain."

It's empty, hollow and good for nothing.

But, again, Christ's RESURRECTION is the core of our confession. We confess: "I believe that Jesus Christ . . . was crucified, died and buried, and on the third day HE ROSE AGAIN from the dead."

What if? What if Jesus had not risen from the dead?

Our preaching is in vain and "your faith is in vain."

And now the apostle adds something else: If Jesus had not risen from the dead:

3. *"You are still in your sins."* v. 17

If Jesus did not conquer death, how could He conquer sin? How could an ordinary man move the mountain of sin that separates us from God? But we are reminded in Romans 4: "Jesus our Lord . . . was put to death for our trespasses AND WAS RAISED for our justification."

Once more we ask, WHAT IF Jesus had not risen from the dead? Paul, inspired by God, writes:

4. *"Then those who have fallen asleep in Christ have perished."* v. 18

If Jesus had not risen from the dead, there would be no hope of ever seeing our loved ones again, those who have died believing Jesus' promise, "Because I live, you shall live also." If Jesus did not rise, they will not rise. We will not rise.

In quick review:

WHAT IF?

WHAT IF Jesus had not risen from the dead?

"Our preaching is in vain."

"Your faith is in vain."

"You are still in your sins."

"Those who have fallen asleep in Christ have perished."

But now all of the "WHAT IFs" are swept away in one great stroke with the glorious proclamation, *"But in fact CHRIST HAS BEEN RAISED FROM THE DEAD . . ."* v. 20.

> He lives, He lives, who once was dead,
> He lives my ever-living Head!

BECAUSE JESUS LIVES our preaching and teaching and reaching is not in vain. Our faith is not in vain. We are no longer in our sins. We shall see our loved ones who have fallen asleep in Jesus.

And not only will we see our loved ones again, but together with them and with angels and archangels and with all the company of heaven we will laud and magnify His glorious name, evermore praising Him and saying:

> *"Blessing and glory and wisdom and thanksgiving and honor and power and might be to our God for ever and ever! Amen."*

God Doesn't Live at Our House

Five-year-old Judy and her brother were frequent visitors in the home of the Smiths who lived next door. One of the things over which Judy pondered in the Smith home was their habit of family prayer at the close of the evening meal.

Every evening, when the Smiths were finished with their supper, Mr. Smith would speak a prayer of thanks, and then the Smith children would each pray a little prayer in turn.

One evening after the Smiths were through eating and Mrs. Smith was getting the dishes ready for washing, she asked little Judy: "Do your parents pray in your home?" Judy shook her head, thought a while, and then replied: "We don't talk to God, because God doesn't live at our house."

She came from a "good home," but in a sense God did not live there. He just wasn't included in the family circle. One question, does God live at your house? Are you on real good talking terms with Him?

The Perpetual Tide

The long, hot and dry summer ebbs. It's like the tide. And like the tide it will return in its appointed cycle.

Ebbing tides expose their undersurface so that as the water runs away, one sees the things that it concealed—sand, seaweed, rocks, shells, including often a conglomerate variety of debris, carelessly discarded—not by nature, not by the fish of the sea, but by untidy, uncaring, careless mankind.

What does the ebbing summer bring to light? Many things. There are, for example, the ongoing everyday things of life. They, however, get little attention. They are hardly noticed. Nevertheless, they are there. And we will see them if only we pay attention. As the summer ebbs, what are some of the things that we see?

All along people were born, and people died. People traveled, and people returned. People worked, and people rested. People loved, and people hated. People fought, and people were reconciled. People looked ahead, and people looked back. Human events and human relationships have gone on, like they usually do, all a part of the natural undersurface of our lives, like the undersurface of the tide. And if we mentally walk around on this extended beach, exposed now by summer's ebbing flow, we can spot these things, pick them up with the fingers of our mind, examine them with curiosity and appreciation, and even tuck them away in the closet of our nature—of our being—and they become part of us.

Inevitably, like the sea, some debris, quite unlovely, gets thrown in, too. In the season's ebb the debris that was carelessly discarded—and is now exposed—spoils the view. One wishes that people had been more careful, had not spread unfounded rumors, had not blackened reputations, had not exploited their fellow human beings' seamier motivations, had not cursed when they should have blessed. These things dirty up the sea of man's existence. How much better if man would control his social littering, promoting instead the more beautiful aspects of his relationships. How much better if we—you and I—would have been more faithful in committing ourselves to that; would have been more faithful in pursuing the habits and practices that preserve the beauty.

Fortunately we get another chance. The tide returns. It can wash the unsightly things away, and the next time the tide goes out, the view will be more pleasant, more Christ-like, more beautiful. What is there for us to do? Only one thing. We join the Psalmist and from the heart plead:

"Have mercy upon me, O God, according to Your lovingkindness; According to the multitude of Your tender mercies, Blot out my transgressions. Wash me thoroughly from my iniquity, And cleanse me from my sin. For I acknowledge my transgressions, And my sin is ever before me. Against You, You only, have I sinned, And done this evil in Your sight—That You may be found just when You speak, and blameless when You judge.

"Behold, I was brought forth in iniquity, And in sin my mother conceived me. Behold, You desire truth in the inward parts, And in the hidden part You will make me to know wisdom.

"Purge me with hyssop, and I shall be clean; Wash me,

and I shall be whiter than snow. Make me to hear joy and gladness, That the bones which You have broken may rejoice. Hide Your face from my sins, And blot out all my iniquities.

"Create in me a clean heart, O God, And renew a steadfast spirit within me. Do not cast me away from Your presence, And do not take Your Holy Spirit from me.

"Restore to me the joy of Your salvation, And uphold me with Your generous Spirit" (Psalm 51:1-12, The New King James Version).

—The lowest ebb is the turn of the tide.—

Come to Calv'ry's holy mountain,
Sinners, ruined by the Fall;
Here a pure and healing fountain
Flows to you, to me, to all,
In a full, PERPETUAL TIDE,
Opened when our Savior died.

Come in poverty and meanness,
Come defiled, without, within;
From infection and uncleanness,
From the leprosy of sin,
Wash your robes and make them white;
Ye shall walk with God in light.

Come in sorrow and contrition,
Wounded, impotent, and blind;
Here the guilty free remission,
Here the troubled peace, may find.
Health this fountain will restore;
He that drinks shall thirst no more.

He that drinks shall live forever;
'Tis a soul-renewing flood.
God is faithful; God will never
Break His covenant of blood,
Signed when our Redeemer died,
Sealed when He was glorified. Amen.

TLH 149

Philippians 1:21

"For to me to live is Jesus,
To die is gain for me."
Whate'er my Savior pleases,
I pray my will shall be.
He is my highest Treasure,
On earth and heav'n above,
He is my highest Pleasure,
My Life,
My Light,
My Love.

God's Own Sacrifice Complete

It is not unusual for us to see the words at the end of an agenda: UNFINISHED BUSINESS. The chairperson oftentimes asks, "Is there some unfinished business?"

On our agendas there may very well be unfinished business, but there is no unfinished business on God's agenda. Regarding His business, God's Son announced from the cross, "IT IS FINISHED!" This being the case, I have entitled our devotion: GOD'S OWN SACRIFICE COMPLETE.

Lent is a season of paradoxical emotions. It is a time to be sorrowful, and also a time to be rejoicing. It is a season of repentance, and also a season of exultation.

During Lent "we who feel the Tempter's power go to dark Gethsemane, follow to the judgment hall and view the Lord of life arraigned; and Calvary's mournful mountain climb to mark the miracle of time": GOD'S OWN SACRIFICE COMPLETE.

During Lent we learn, in a most penetrating way, to confess with the Apostle Paul: "He loved me and gave Himself for me!" We hear our blessed Savior cry out: "It is finished!" And that tells us that "the strife is over, the battle done."

We hear the Easter angel proclaim: "He is risen!"—and that affirms: "Now is the Victor's triumph won. Now be the song of praise begun. Alleluia!"

Lent is the time when none of us should be permitted to escape the pointing and accusing finger of the Law which says, "You killed the Prince of Life." No one has understood the meaning of Lent until he is able to say from the heart: "Ah! I also and my sin wrought Thy deep affliction; This indeed the cause hath been of Thy crucifixion."

Lent tells us that we are free in Christ; that we are free from sin's guilt, for Christ was declared guilty by God FOR US. Lent tells us that we are free from sin's punishment, since God held His Son accountable for OUR sins. Lent tells us that we are free from sin's rule because Christ has broken sin's power over us.

But we are more than "free from." We are "free to." We are free to love God by loving our neighbor. We are free to serve God, not for the purpose of establishing righteousness of our own; but free to serve the Lord because He is our RIGHTEOUSNESS and He is our Peace.

When God sacrificed His Son on the altar of the Cross, He went all the way. It is complete. "It is finished!" There is NO UNFINISHED BUSINESS ON GOD'S AGENDA, except for us to witness to GOD'S OWN SACRIFICE COMPLETE.

"It is finished!" He will keep us
In His precious blood-bought love.
Now the Hallelujah Chorus
Can reverberate above.
It is done! Thank God 'tis done!
Christ has our salvation won!

Making the Most of Pentecost

The story of the first Pentecost is thrilling and exciting. We are not thinking so much of the outward manifestations that accompanied the descent of the Holy Spirit, though they were, indeed, most startling. Rather, we are thinking of the tremendous effect that the outpouring of the Holy Spirit had upon the followers of our Lord and Savior.

Up until that time they were such a weak lot. The record gives the impression of people bewildered and mystified by their experiences. If we try to put ourselves in their place, perhaps we would have no difficulty in understanding that. They had witnessed mighty miracles. They had run the gamut of emotions. They had received promises so great as to be almost incomprehensible. They had received orders to do things that apparently lay far beyond their abilities and capacities.

However, with the coming of the Holy Spirit there was an abrupt transformation. The situation was clarified. Confusion and bewilderment disappeared. The transcendent import of what they had seen and heard was grasped. Divine promises were taken at their face value. Divine orders became the dominant influence in their lives.

In so many ways we Christians today are like those disciples *before* Pentecost. Things have happened and continue to take place that leave us in a daze. We read what the Lord has promised and we seem unable to put much stock in His assurances. We know what He has commanded, but oftentimes we lack the courage to tackle the job in an "all-out" manner. Face to face with pressing problems, the Church frequently flounders and tumbles.

We venture the assertion that one reason for this lamentable condition is the failure of so many of us to grasp the gift of the Holy Spirit which the Lord would bestow upon us. Instead, programs, systems, organizations, committees—these are relied on. And God will not do His work that way. These are not His means. Therefore we so often fail.

MAKING THE MOST OF PENTECOST means that we faithfully, diligently, prayerfully seek for a rich and abundant measure of God's Spirit; that we indefatigably dig into the Holy Scriptures, and that we faithfully frequent the Lord's Altar for the sustenance our souls need; that deterred by no hindrances we avail ourselves of every opportunity to deepen our spiritual lives and faithfully, diligently to exercise them. Only then shall we twentieth century believers be able to repeat what the first century Church did.

Creator Spirit, heav'nly dove,
Descend upon us from above;
With graces manifold restore
Your creatures as they were before.

Praise we the Father and the Son
And Holy Spirit, with them one;
And may the Son on us bestow
The gifts that from the Spirit flow.   LW 156:1,7

Three P's in a Pod
(Protection, Power, Presence)

There are times when we all need encouragement. Because of our frail, sinful nature we become discouraged, disappointed, and sometimes we slip near the brink of despair.

What can lift our souls in times like these? Really, it's not what, but rather, who? To some extent other believers can help. However, the real encouragement and strength comes from the holy Lord God Himself. The Psalmist reminds us of this when in Psalm 46:1ff. he writes: *"God is our Refuge and Strength, a very present help in trouble . . . The Lord of hosts is with us; the God of Jacob is our Refuge."* And in the explanation of the First Article of the Apostles' Creed we confess of the Lord: "He defends me against all danger, guards and protects me from all evil."

Let us note the first "P" in the Pod.

THE PROTECTION OF THE LORD

When David wrote: "God is our Refuge," he may well have been thinking of the seven cities of refuge to which a person could flee for protection. In God, however, we have a far greater Refuge.

When we are weary we can flee to Him, any time day or night, and find rest for our weary souls. When we are tossed to and fro, we can find in Jesus *"the peace of God that passes all understanding" (Phil. 4:7).* When we have doubts and fears, He will calm our troubled hearts and minds and give us joy, even in the midst of trials. When our sins cause us alarm, we can flee to the Lord and there find in Him "peace that knows no measure, and joys that thro' all time abide."

Oh, yes, God is our Refuge, and not some place or city. The holy, loving, eternal God Himself is our Protection. Therefore we joyfully confess:

Whom should I give my heart's affection
But Thee, who givest Thine to faith?
Thy fervent love is my protection;
Lord, Thou hast loved me unto death.
My heart with Thine shall ever be
One heart throughout eternity. Amen.

TLH 404:4

Abide with Thy protection
Among us, Lord, our Strength,
Lest world and Satan fell us
And overcome at length.

TLH 53:5

The Psalmist not only says that God is our Refuge, our Protection, but adds, "and strength," power.

THE POWER OF THE LORD

Certainly, the Lord was Joseph's strength to overcome temptation in Potiphar's house. He was Moses' power to deliver the people of Israel out of bondage. He was David's strength and power over the giant. He was Elijah's power over the false prophets. He was the Apostle Paul's power and strength to stand firm and to preach the glorious Gospel even at the expense of his life.

Without question, the Lord God has been the power of every believer in every age, and He will continue to be our Strength—our Power. And He who declares, *"All power is given to Me in heaven and on earth"* (Matt. 28:18), will never leave us or forsake us.

We therefore plea:

Thou seest my feebleness;
Jesus, be Thou my Pow'r,
My Help and Refuge in distress,
My Fortress and my Tow'r.

TLH 433:3

David declares, "God is our Refuge (Protection), He is our Strength (Power)," and now the third "P."

THE PRESENCE OF THE LORD

The Psalmist says of the Lord, He is "a very present help in trouble." He abides with us. He dwells with us and in us. He promises, *"I am with you always, even to the end of the age" (Matt. 28:20).* He assures us that He will never leave us or forsake us. Others may leave, but He remains.

Our gracious and mighty God is not some far-off source from whom we can seek advice in our troubled times in life, but He is a very present help. He is the omnipresent One. There is never a place and never a time when He is not present in all His glorious Person. He is as near as our heart's desire and our troubled soul's cry. He is truly *"a God at hand . . ." (Jer. 23:23).*

God, our God, has been faithful throughout history to sustain, protect, empower and bless His people, and He assures us that His presence shall go with us, and *"in His*

228

presence there is fullness of joy, and at His right hand pleasures forevermore" (Ps. 16:11).

May we ever heed the invitation of the Psalmist to faithfully come before the *presence* of the Lord in worship and praise. Yes, let us long to *dwell in His presence* now and forevermore, confessing:

I need Thy *presence* every passing hour;
What but Thy grace can foil the Tempter's power?
Who like Thyself my guide and stay can be?
Through cloud and sunshine, oh, abide with me!

TLH 552:6

Redeemer, come! I open wide
My heart to Thee; here, Lord, abide!
Let me Thine inner presence feel,
Thy grace and love in me reveal;
Thy Holy Spirit guide us on
Until our glorious goal is won.
Eternal praise and fame
We offer to Thy name. Amen.

TLH 73:5

There we have THREE P's IN A POD—Protection, Power, Presence; attributes possessed in their fullness only in the Lord Jesus Christ, and freely, fully offered to us all through Word and Sacraments.

A Recipe and Rules
for a Happy Home

1969 American Mother of the Year
Mrs. R. G. LeTourneau

I have something on my heart that I want to say to you young people—something so important that I wish I could find a way to say it that would catch your attention. But all I can do is to say it simply and sincerely and hope that it finds a response.

I have often repeated the statement, "The family that prays together stays together," and I believe that is true. Since I, as 1969 American Mother of the Year, have worked with the Young Mothers Council Service, I have realized the need for another emphasis. That is that "praying together" must begin before the marriage if the full blessing of that practice is to be realized.

So, to young people who are looking forward to marriage and the establishment of a home, I want to say you should make sure, before marriage, that it will be possible for you to truly become "one in the Lord."

How I wish I could talk to each of you, not just before the wedding or after the marriage, but before the engagement. The Scripture raises the question, *"Can two walk together except they be agreed?" (Amos 3:3).* That does not mean there will be no differences in opinions, judgments or desires, but it does mean that there must be a foundation for agreement that makes it possible to

230

resolve the problems that are so common to life. If you are planning to live together for life, you had better establish a solid foundation on which to build. It is obvious that you won't pray together unless both of you have put your faith in Christ for salvation. That, in itself, establishes the first prerequisite for a happy home—that both of you are children of God.

I believe, however, that praying together about your relationship and the home you are looking forward to will reveal if both of you are *possessing* Christians or only *professing* Christians. I also think it will not be possible to pray together without realizing that you must get into the Word of God together. If you take this counsel to heart, your courtship days will become much more meaningful.

Some may think good health is an absolute necessity for happiness. Some may think a measure of wealth is the prerequisite. Some may think freedom from sorrow is demanded. Some may think reverses cannot be included in happiness. But life seems to teach us that none of these guarantees nor do they rule out happiness.

There is a prerequisite to happiness and that is the only guarantee, because it rests, not upon circumstances ROUND us but upon circumstances WITHIN us. Consider these words from the Bible: *"Delight yourselves in the Lord; yes, find your joy in Him at all times. Have a reputation for gentleness, and never forget the nearness of your Lord. Don't worry over anything whatever; tell God every detail of your needs in earnest and thankful prayer, and the peace of God, which transcends human understanding, will keep constant guard over your hearts and minds as they rest in Christ Jesus"* (Phil. 4:4-7, Translation by J. Phillips).

Five Rules for a Happy Home

No. 1 FAMILY DEVOTIONS

There should be a time each day when father and mother gather the children together and either read a selection in a good devotional book or some passage in the Bible. If the children are very small, use a Bible story book suited to their level. Make it interesting for their age. Then have prayer with them.

No. 2 LOVING CONSISTENT DISCIPLINE

A child will feel very frustrated, unloved and unwanted if not disciplined. To be effective, discipline must be consistent and must be administered with love.

No. 3 TAKE THE CHILDREN TO CHURCH AND SUNDAY SCHOOL

TAKE the children to Sunday school and to church. Don't SEND them. Become involved. That family that is involved in the church is more likely to stay together.

No. 4 AFFECTION

Affection between mother and father and between parents and children is so very important. The greatest thing you can leave your children is not money or things, but rather the knowledge that mother and father love each other. This creates a sense of security.

Don't take each other for granted. Let the children know that you love them. Tell them so. Commend them when they are good, kind and thoughtful. Take an interest in the things that interest them. It will work miracles.

No. 5 Don't Criticize

Seek opportunities for commendation. This applies to members of the family, but also to your pastor, Sunday school teachers and public school teachers. Teach your children to emphasize the positive rather than the negative.

Try looking for something to praise. We can always find something to criticize in anyone if that is what we are looking for, BUT we can find something to praise in anyone if we look for it. If at times you have to criticize someone, it should be done in private and in a spirit of love and understanding. Parents should never criticize each other in the presence of the children. Criticizing and faultfinding is a bad habit and very contagious.

Best wishes for a happy home,

Mrs. R. G. LeTourneau

Together we use God's Word,
Together we grow in Christ,
Together we love all mankind,
Together we serve our God,
Together we hope for heaven,
These are our hopes and ideals.
Help us to attain them, O God,
Through Jesus Christ, our Lord.

"Children may mess up a house, but adults break up a home."

"Remember, when your child has a tantrum, don't have one of your own."

A New Year's Eve Dream

Around thirty years ago an article appeared in the LLL publication entitled, "A New Year's Eve Dream." With some adaptations and revisions, I would like to share it with you on this New Year's Eve, with the hope and prayer that it will help us to bid farewell to an old year and to welcome in the new.

The New Year's Eve service was over. It had been solemn and a bit sad, as it always is. No one likes to say the last "Good-bye" to an old friend—and after twelve months the year is like an old friend.

Toward midnight there would be a quiet, little get-together with friends. I sat down near the Christmas tree briefly to review the outstanding events of the departing year. From the warmth of the room and from sheer exhaustion—it happened, as it usually does when I sit still for a while—I fell asleep.

Then came the dream. In this dream I was part of a large crowd, nervously milling in front of a custom-house. You were in the crowd, too, and everybody I know and millions more. Each of us was carrying a little heart-shaped grip, the significance of which at first made no impression on me. I began to examine the outside of my grip and where I expected to find the name of the country we were about to enter, there were four large numbers: 1967.

As I began to worry how long it would take for all of us to pass through customs, a friendly officer stepped up and addressed us all:

Ladies, gentlemen, boys and girls: Welcome to 1967! This is not an ordinary port of entry. You will not be asked to open your grips nor to declare your possessions. We charge no duty here; we simply advise you. In a moment you will have an opportunity to repack and re-arrange the contents of your grips. If you ignore our instructions and insist on taking items against which we advise, duty will be collected throughout the year in terms of disappointment, frustration, anxiety, fear and the like.

We know from experience that many of you carry greeting cards wishing you "A Happy and Prosperous New Year." While it is good to know that friends think kindly of us, their soft and tender wishes will mean absolutely nothing in the land you are about to enter. This is pioneer country. For the most part you will be traveling through uncharted areas. We hope that your trip will be most enjoyable, but we can give you no assurance that it will be. There will be many days with varied experiences. You will, no doubt, be called upon to make a lot of decisions and to solve quite an array of problems. You may come upon a long series of days and nights that are severely trying. They may include tragedy, reverses, pain and sorrow.

Since this will be the case, we suggest that you clear your grips of all meaningless wishes for happiness and prosperity; all dreams of ease and comfort and luxury; and make sure you have the tools with which to fashion a good and useful life, come sunshine or storm.

Very likely some of you imagine you carry security with you in the form of check books, purses, health insurance, credit cards, etc. We will have to remind you that there is no absolute security in any of these. You need something unfailing and dependable. And this kind of security is a matter of the heart.

I would like to point you to an unfailing source of guidance, strength and comfort as you begin Journey 1967. I would simply point you to the Tour Guide, Christ the Lord He knows the way. To Him the future is as an open book. There is nothing hidden from Him. When you are confused and do not know how to proceed, He will say to you, "Follow Me, I know the way." When you are weary and nervous, lonely and forsaken, He will promise, "I will be with you always." When you feel guilty and terribly ashamed, He will assure you, "I forgive you." When you feel weak and powerless to cope with forces that threaten to hurt you, make you miserable, destroy you, He will remind you, "All power is given to Me in heaven and on earth." "Don't let your heart be troubled, neither let it be afraid."

Indications are that most of you will actually have a good journey in 1967. I hope you will have the good sense to accept it humbly and gratefully. This will be a good year for you to develop and to strengthen the fibers of your soul—and for loving service to God and to one another. It will be a journey of opportunity for you; opportunity to "grow in grace and in the knowledge of the Lord"; opportunity to "serve the Lord with gladness"; and opportunity to become more Christlike, more loving, patient, understanding and forgiving.

Now you will all have a few moments to go through and examine what you have in your grip, that heart-shaped one. What are you taking into this new country? Is there perhaps some bitterness, some discontent, a chip on the shoulder; is there perhaps some anger, some ill-feeling toward someone? Are you carrying a loveless attitude? To make certain that you won't be dragging any of this "dead weight" along, I suggest that you turn your grips completely over in order that every speck of bitterness and sin may drop out. Get rid of all of it!

Now repack. Don't put back containers with the acids of hatred, jealousy, pride, anger, fear or guilt. It's hard to keep them bottled up. They have a way of spilling out over everything. They can make your bodies sick, warp your minds, scar and destroy your souls. Away with all such things! Those nasty old habits, put them off. Don't drag them along. While you are discarding, be certain to throw away the objects that brought embarrassment to others. Resolve to bury them. You may be tempted to make bad jokes of them and hurt someone.

Keep the habit of forgetting unpleasant things; things that disorganize your life and develop the tendency to remember kindnesses and to look for the good in others. "Whatsoever things are true, whatsoever things are honest, whatsoever things are just, whatsoever things are pure, whatsoever things are lovely, whatsoever things are of good report; if there be any virtue, and if there be any praise, think on these things." (Phil. 4:8f.)

Don't be embarrassed to carry along a box of sentiments that remind you of your better moments. And by the way, take along a good measure of compliments which you will want to pass out freely. Most important, stay close to your Tour Guide. Trust

Him implicitly for everything.

And now, with your past confessed and forgiven; with a cleansed heart—cleansed in the blood of the Lamb of God—trusting solely in our blessed Lord and Savior, let us pray:

O Lord,
Before the cross subdued we bow,
To You our prayers addressing,
Recounting all Your mercies now,
And all our sins confessing;
Beseeching You this coming year
To keep us in Your faith and fear
And crown us with Your blessing.

And now, it's no longer a dream you see—it's real, very real. Only a few more precious hours and, by God's grace, we will begin this new journey labeled 1967.

- A.C.O.

Then, O great God, in years to come,
Whatever may betide us,
Right onward through our journey home
Be Thou at hand to guide us;
Nor leave us till at close of life,
Safe from all perils, toil, and strife,
Heaven shall enfold and hide us. Amen.

TLH 110:6

Office Upstairs

Someone told this story of the old doctor who was a very fine Christian and a very useful man. He did not have a swanky office. He had only two or three small rooms on the second floor of a building, at the head of a flight of stairs. On the street below was this sign:

DR. THOMAS RILEY
OFFICE UPSTAIRS

One day the doctor was missing. They found him dead in his office. A few nights before he had gone out into a wintry storm on a call. He had taken cold and died.

When his friends buried him they wanted to perpetuate his memory in the best possible way. They wondered what sort of stone to put over his grave.

What meaningful epitaph could they put on the stone? They thought of his faithful labors of love motivated by his loving faith in the Lord Jesus Christ.

One of his friends took the old battered sign and put it upon the doctor's grave. It simply read,

DR. THOMAS RILEY
OFFICE UPSTAIRS
and pointed it heavenward.

Hold Thou Thy cross before my closing eyes,
Shine through the gloom, and point me to the skies.
Heaven's morning breaks,
   and earth's vain shadows flee;
In life, in death, O Lord, abide with me! Amen.

TLH 552:8

Sit a Spell

The other day as I was making some calls, one of our members invited me to come in and "sit a spell." I will have to admit that I had never heard that expression before.

However, before we can stand up, really stand up, it is necessary that we "sit a spell." Martha went into the kitchen. She stood. Mary made another choice. She chose to "sit a spell." And Jesus made it abundantly clear that Mary made the wise choice.

Before we stand, we must sit. Before we can serve our Lord, we must be served by our Lord. Before we speak for Him, we must listen to Him. We, in other words, must "sit a spell." If we are to be alive and to live, He must live in us.

Where does the Lord live?

First, He lives in His Word and His Sacraments. These are His vehicles for the action of His Spirit upon the hearts and lives of folks—both big ones and little ones, old ones and young ones.

He needs no organizations, no committees, no documents, no conferences, conventions or convocations. He needs no sword.

> He conquers by loving.
> He saves by serving.
> He overpowers by wooing.
> He demands by leading.

He gives life by dying and
by rising again.
And He confers what He is and
what He has done by precious
means—the Means of Grace,
His Word and Sacraments.

Our living, loving Lord lives and acts by means of His holy, inspired, Spirit-filled, power-packed Word.

That is what Mary chose. We are told *"Mary sat at the Lord's feet and listened to His teachings" (Luke 10:39).* She made the right choice and the Lord said so.

Listen to the Lord: *"Martha, Martha, you are anxious and troubled about many things; one thing is needful. Mary has chosen the good portion, which shall not be taken away from her" (Luke 10:41f.).*

And so we Christian teachers who would rise to the challenges of the day and who would stand fast and firm in the Lord, need to choose "the one thing needful" as did Mary. We need to "sit a spell" so that He who lives in Word and Sacrament would live in our hearts and lives. Only then are we truly able to "stand up for Jesus" and teach, really teach!

Gracious God and Lord,
help us to "sit a spell"
that we, Your holy Word
may faithfully tell. Amen.

One Nation Under God

(written in the 60's)

What does USA mean to you?—spiring mountains and fertile valleys?—rolling plains and the scent of new mown hay?—sooty cities and industrial greatness? Yes, and likely much more. America is a country that evokes a sense of pride, security and patriotism. America is more, much more than sights and sounds and smells.

Can all that America is and means be an accident? It's hard to see how. The pilgrim fathers and mothers moved here because they believed they were directed by the guiding hand of Almighty God. We, as a nation, have been a very favored people. Why are we so blessed? Could it be because our nation was founded as a Christian nation with faith in the Lord Jesus Christ?

Nations are composed of individuals. Ordinary people related to God often become extraordinary people. Many of our founding fathers and mothers were such people. The Mayflower Compact, the Continental Congress, the Declaration of Independence, each acknowledge ONE NATION UNDER GOD. Stamped on our coins and printed on our bills are the familiar words: IN GOD WE TRUST.

Being A NATION UNDER GOD means we look to the Almighty for direction, protection and blessing. The pilgrims are often pictured on their way to church. In one hand is a musket and in the other is a Bible. A NATION UNDER GOD realizes His justice. Let's face it, God does not belong to us exclusively and He will not be used by us. If we act motivated by aggression, hatred and self-interest, God will judge us. No nation ever gets God on its side. THE NATION MUST COME ON GOD'S SIDE!

THE NATION UNDER GOD seeks His guidance. Individuals need to seek God's leadership for their lives, and leaders of nations need God's wisdom in making decisions of national and worldwide significance. The leaders need to be led. God has guided us this far, often in spite of ourselves. We need to actively seek His direction for our future.

We call ourselves A NATION UNDER GOD. This is a basic principle of our national foundation and future. If God is to continue to prosper our beloved nation, we need to act like we are A NATION UNDER GOD.

It might be well for us to be reminded of some statements by our forebears. George Washington: "It is impossible to govern the nation without the Bible." Andrew Jackson: "The Bible is the rock on which this republic rests." Abraham Lincoln: "If God has a place and work for me, and I believe He has, I believe I'm ready. I am nothing, but truth is everything. I know I am right because I know that liberty is right, for Christ teaches it, and Christ is God." Woodrow Wilson: "We are now living on the interest from the spiritual investments of our forefathers." Herbert Hoover: "Our church and religious institutions are indispensable stabilizing factors in our civilization."

Dwight D. Eisenhower was responsible for the addition of the words UNDER GOD in the Pledge of Allegiance. During his second inauguration he placed his hand on the Bible and read aloud from the Bible: *"If My people, which are called by My name, shall humble themselves, and pray, and seek My face, and turn from their wicked ways; then will I hear from heaven, and will forgive their sin, and will heal their land"* (1 Chr. 7:14).

O America, in the passage above we have God's answer, solution and promise for this great nation of ours. Read it again and again, remembering that YOU ARE AMERICA—ONE NATION UNDER GOD!

Watch and Pray for the Lord's Return

(written in the late 50's)

When the special assistant to the postmaster general in Washington, D.C., answered a telephone call the other day, he received a request that a commemorative stamp for the second coming of Christ be issued.

Needless to say, the postal officer was somewhat caught off guard for an immediate answer. Finally, however, he suggested to the caller: "If you will tell me the exact time and place of the second coming of Christ, we will see what can be done about issuing a commemorative stamp." The caller hung up.

Later on, this special assistant, who is also the public relations chief for the post office department, related the incident to newsmen in Kansas City, Missouri. They, of course, published it. The result? The chief received a dozen letters from readers who said they knew the time and place of the Lord's return.

However, the postal department is still holding out because the dates are all different—ranging from July 1961 to the year 2061!

There certainly can be no doubt of the fact of our Lord's return, for He states: *"I will come again."* And we know the Lord is Truth personified and *"cannot lie" (Titus 1:2)*.

What is more, the manner of the Lord's coming is revealed in these inspired words: *"The Lord Himself shall* descend from heaven with a shout, with the voice of the archangel, and with the trump of God: and the dead in Christ shall rise first: then we (the believers) which are alive and remain shall be caught up together with them in the clouds, to meet the Lord in the air: and so shall we ever be with the Lord" (1 Thess. 4:16-17).

The suddenness of the Lord's coming is stated thus: *"In a moment, in the twinkling of an eye, at the last trump: for the trumpet shall sound, and the dead shall be raised incorruptible, and we shall be changed"* (1 Cor. 15:52).

And in all three Creeds of Christendom, The Apostles', The Nicene and The Athanasian, we unequivocally confess our blessed Savior's "return to judge the living and the dead."

The one thing that is not revealed, however, is the date of the Lord's return. No human being knows the day nor the hour when He will fulfill His promise to come again. *"Watch therefore,"* we are urged, *"for you do not know on what day your Lord is coming"* (Matt. 24:42). *"Watch, therefore, for you know neither the day nor the hour."* (Matt. 25:13, Mark 13:32-37, Luke 21:36 and Acts 20:31)

The Holy Scriptures instruct, encourage and advise: *"Remember then what you received and heard; keep that, and repent. If you will not awake, I WILL COME like a thief, and you will not know at what hour I WILL COME UPON YOU"* (Rev. 3:3).

When the Thessalonians heard the Gospel of Christ, how that Christ died for our sins, was buried, rose again, ascended to heaven and promised to return, they believed it. We are told that they *"turned to God from idols to serve the living and true God; and to wait for His Son from heaven, whom He raised from the dead, even Jesus, who delivered us from the wrath to come" (1 Thess. 1:9-10).*

No question about it, the Thessalonians believed that the Lord would most certainly return on the Last Day. What about us? What about you? Are we faithfully watching and waiting for our blessed Savior's return? Are we ready? Are we prepared to meet Him?

I'm reminded of the teacher who, one morning, announced to the girls and boys that the superintendent was coming to their school, though he did not know the exact time. He asked that everything be in order, and that everyone be ready to meet the superintendent.

All the girls and boys began to clean their desks, straighten the books, pick things up from the floor, etc., except one little girl who continued with her coloring project seemingly quite oblivious to the announcement and the request of the teacher.

When the teacher asked her to join the other children in getting ready for the coming of the superintendent, she said that she would do it the next day. "But what if the superintendent comes today?" the teacher asked. "Oh, then I'll do it this afternoon, right after lunch." "But what if the superintendent comes this morning?" the teacher asked. "Oh," the little girl responded, "I better get everything cleaned up and put into order right now and then keep it that way!" She would be ready!

Interesting as a commemorative stamp would be, it is not going to be issued. *"Of that day and hour no one knows, not even the angels in heaven, nor the Son, but the Father only."* (Matt. 24:36, Mark 13:32) *"As the lightening comes from the east and shines as far as the west, so will be the coming of the Son of man."* (Matt. 24:27)

Like that little girl, let us get everything regarding our hearts and lives cleaned up and straightened out now, and then, through the cleansing power of the Holy Spirit, keep it that way. Yes, let us watch and pray for the Lord's return!

We have our Savior's blessed promise: "Behold, I come quickly!" May we confidently and joyfully respond with the last prayer of the Bible: "EVEN SO, COME, LORD JESUS!" AMEN!

O'er the distant mountains breaking
Comes the redd'ning dawn of day.
Rise, my soul, from sleep awaking;
Rise and sing and watch and pray.
'Tis thy Savior, 'Tis thy Savior,
On His bright returning way.

Nearer is my soul's salvation;
Spent the night, the day at hand.
Keep me in my lowly station,
Watching for Thee till 1 stand,
O my Savior, O my Savior,
In Thy bright, Thy promised, land.

With my lamp well trimmed and burning,
Swift to hear and slow to roam,
Watching for Thy glad returning
To restore me to my home.
Come, my Savior, Come, my Savior,
O my Savior, quickly come. Amen.

TLH 606:1,3,4

Amen, Amen, Amen

Back in 1950 a small group of people living in the village of Weston, Illinois, asked if I would consider conducting Sunday evening services for them. Besides some large grain elevators, there was a combination general store and post office, a community building, and a little white church in the village. Over the years a number of different denominations held services in that church, the last being my predecessor at St. Paul Lutheran Church, Chenoa, Illinois.

Accepting their invitation proved to be a very interesting experience. While a few folks came to the church in their pick-up trucks, most of them lived nearby and walked to the church with their pet dogs. While several dogs remained outside during the service waiting for their masters, three or four were brought inside and sat very quietly beside their owners.

In the pews were song books, *Tabernacle Hymns, No. 2*. Since I was not familiar with the book, I asked if they had a favorite song to begin our first service together. Any number of song titles were called out, the loudest being Number 148, the song "Life's Railway to Heaven." The first verse goes as follows:

Life is like a mountain railroad,
With an engineer that's brave;
We must make the run successful,
From the cradle to the grave;
Watch the curves, the fills, the tunnels;
Never falter, never quail;
Keep your hand upon the throttle,
And your eyes upon the rail.

Chorus: Blessed Savior, Thou will guide us
Till we reach that blissful shore;
Where the angels wait to join us
In Thy praise forevermore.

As we were coming to the end of the first verse I tried to get the attention of the pianist to bring the train to a halt. However, she was going up and down those keys gaining speed with each line! Obviously she was really living the line that appeared in all four verses: "Keep your hand upon the throttle, and your eyes upon the rail." Fearing I might cause a train wreck by throwing a switch, I decided to try to "hang on" through all four verses.

The final verse:

As you roll across the trestle,
Spanning Jordan's swelling tide;
You behold the Union Depot
Into which your train will glide;
There you'll meet the Superintendent,
God the Father, God the Son,
With hearty joyous plaudits,
"Weary pilgrim, welcome home."

With that sometimes reckless, jolting ride, needless to say, I made it a point to select the songs after that!

However, there was another "surprise" awaiting me. These were "Amen!" people. Once I got into my sermon they "cheered me on" with their shouts of "Amen, Amen, brother, Amen and Amen!" These folks lived an "Amen" life. Do we? Do you?

The word, AMEN, is used in several ways in the Bible. It is a Hebrew word meaning "firm" and "certainly," and is sometimes used to express approval, meaning "Pray it be so." It also was used by Jesus to give emphasis to His words and is translated as "Verily." However, most commonly AMEN is used at the end of prayers to confirm the words and mark the finish of a prayer, a practice started by worshippers in the Early Church.

The word, AMEN, is used in many languages. AMEN is much more than a spiritual period at the end of a prayer; rather, it's a clear, decisive declaration of faith on the part of a believer, saying, "Amen, God, what I have just sung or said to You, this is true."

In the old Catechism, page 169, and the new Catechism, p. 195, we have the explanation to the end of The Lord's Prayer, the model prayer of all believers in the Lord Jesus Christ: "That I should be certain that these petitions are acceptable to our Father in Heaven, and are heard by Him; for He Himself has commanded us so to pray, and has promised to hear us. Amen, Amen, that is, Yes, Yes, it shall be so." If you were to paraphrase that in the vernacular, you might say, "Without a doubt, this is absolutely true!"

Following are some Bible texts listed from Cruden's Concordance to the King James Version of the Bible in which the word, AMEN is used:

Num. 5:22	Deut. 27:15	1 Kings 1:36
1 Chr. 16:36	Ps. 41:13	Ps. 72:19
Ps. 89:52	Ps. 106:48	Jer. 28:6
Matt. 6:13	1 Cor. 14:6	2 Cor. 1:20

Several years ago the editor of The Lutheran Layman's League publication wrote: "I have wondered why we sing so many hymns today without concluding with 'Amen,' especially when most hymns are prayers to God.

"It appears to me that a proper perspective is needed when we approach God's throne in song, too. 'Amen' gives us that perspective. When, at the close of a hymn of praise or repentance we sing an 'Amen,' we are saying, 'We really mean it, God. This is true.'

"However, of greater importance, is your life one big 'Amen'? Do you ask God, through the power of the Holy Spirit, to make your life acceptable to Him? Do you wish to draw closer to Him?

"Do you aim to change sinful, wayward practices and habits which have wedged themselves between you and your relationship with God? Do you wish to bow to His will and ways at all times, in all things? That's the meaning of an 'Amen' life!

"Too many times even the best Christians live an 'Ah, me' life. Take it easy; live it up; enjoy, enjoy, enjoy; put yourself first; don't reach out to others if it costs you. An 'Ah, me' life seems grand when I'm in the center. That, however, is the attitude that alienates. That is the aim that never hits a God-pleasing target.

"Don't drop your 'Amen' from prayers and hymns. Let your life through the Spirit be a continuous 'Amen,' acknowledging the kingship and glory and grace of God in Christ Jesus and showing that attitude of faith and servanthood as you live every day in His love and to His glory and praise."

Praise to the Lord!
Oh, let all that is in me adore Him!
All that hath life and breath,
come now with praises before Him!
Let the AMEN
Sound from His people again;
Gladly for aye we adore Him. AMEN.

TLH 39:5

No other word fits better here than AMEN, AMEN, AMEN!

Heavenly Father, each morning are new
Mercies abundant all flowing from You.

We Pray

Undeserved of Your goodness though we be,
We know full well that Your blessings are free.
You provide all needs of body and soul;
Our hearts we would lift and our praise extol.
Give, we pray, Your Holy Spirit to us,
That to You we give thanks from dawn to dusk.
Grant, now, in the name and strength of Your Son,
We live to serve You 'til our days are done.
AMEN.

Lord, while we pray, we lift our eyes

To dear ones gone before us,
Safe home with You in paradise,
Whose peace descends upon us;
And be with You, when life is past,
To reunite us all at last
With those who've gone before us.
AMEN.